to be continued...

EDITED BY MICHELE KARLSBERG
AND KAREN X. TULCHINSKY

Firebrand
Books

Book and cover design by Nightwood
Cover photograph by Jess Wells

Printed in Canada

10 9 8 7 6 5 4 3 2 1

Library of Congress Cataloging-in-Publication Data

To be continued— / edited by Michele Karlsberg and Karen X. Tulchinsky.
    p.   cm.
    ISBN 1-56341-104-0 (paper : alk. paper). —ISBN 1-56341-105-9
(cloth : alk. paper)
    1. Lesbians—Fiction. 2. Lesbians' writings, American. 3. Short stories,
American—Women authors. I. Karlsberg, Michele. II. Tulchinsky, Karen X.
PS648.L47T6   1998
813'.01089206643—dc21   98-39764
                                                              CIP

ACKNOWLEDGMENTS

Karen X. Tulchinsky: Your editorial suggestions, as well as your wisdom and experience in the areas of writing and publishing, have been invaluable to me.

Nancy K. Bereano: Thank you for making a dream come true.

The writers included in the collection: Thank you for the work that you do, the words you eloquently present, and for sharing the stories that need to be heard.

The late Stan Leventhal: You introduced me to the world of lesbian and gay books, and I will continue to introduce the world to these books, in your footsteps.

Richard LaBonte: You always give me the opportunity to soar, thank you.

Allison and Heather Karlsberg, Mom, Grandma, and Aunt Jay: First, put down V.C. Andrews; *To Be Continued...* is your next read. Thank you for providing me with two gifts that I don't take for granted—love and acceptance.

Latifah A. Rabb, Robert Kelly, Steven Cotugno, Lisa Pilkington, Lorraine Donald, Hazel Brown, Pedro Perez, and Valerie Sagaria: Your support, friendship, encouragement, advice, love, and enthusiasm have been precious to me.

Earnestine Lannigan: You give me strength and faith each and every day of my life. Your unconditional love allows me to be myself, and I thank you for that. The whole world should be lucky enough to share your friendship.

Michele Karlsberg

Many thanks to Nancy Bereano for her encouragement, and to the women of Firebrand Books for their enthusiasm, hard work, and expertise in bringing this book to publication.

Thanks to Michele Karlsberg for the great idea, signing on the incredible authors, marketing expertise, and friendship.

Thanks to my friends, family, and colleagues for assistance, support, and encouragement: Lee McArthur, Maike Engelbrecht, Della McCreary, James Johnstone, Barbara Kuhne, Dianne Whelan, Brian Lam, Blaine Kyllo, Rachel Pepper, Nisa Donnelly, Arlene Tully, Tova Fox, Lois Fine, Marlys La Brash, Trigger, Richard Banner, Victoria Chan.

Thanks to Jess Wells for the front-cover photography and editors' photo.

Arigato to my fiancée, Terrie Akemi Hamazaki, for her love, patience, and unflinching faith in me, and to Charlie Tulchinsky-Hamazaki for his own special brand of unconditional love.

Karen X. Tulchinsky

NOTES FROM THE EDITORS

FROM MICHELE KARLSBERG:

Three years ago, I began thinking about what I could give to the reading public in addition to the publicity and marketing work that I do to promote lesbian and gay books. Helping to create a terrific book from the ground up was the answer. I am not a writer, so it would not be a book of my stories; instead, a book of stories by the writers I have worked with and admired over the years. And not just another anthology on the shelves. This would be something different. Something new and intriguing.

We all know that each and every one of our days gives us a story, but tomorrow always brings more. Some days are more exciting than others. We have no idea what to expect, thus living a life full of our own personal cliffhangers. What about a book of stories that are like life: exciting, unpredictable, filled with characters who live each day to the fullest, and leave us wanting to know more. I held my thoughts and ideas until the time was right, until I knew I had the perfect editorial partner to share my enthusiasm. Along came Karen X. Tulchinsky, who gave me the spark I needed to get this project on the road.

A dream has now become a reality, and it is with great pleasure that I get to share this dream with you, the reader. If you have read any books by the writers included in this collection, you will know exactly why I think highly of their work. If you are not already familiar with their writing, welcome to a world of literary excellence. I hope that you will continue to read their work with pleasure.

FROM KAREN X. TULCHINSKY:

Michele Karlsberg and I met early in 1996 while she was working with my publishers to promote the recently released anthology I had co-edited, *Queer View Mirror: Lesbian & Gay Short Short Fiction.* In a subsequent conversation Michele told me of an idea she had for an anthology of lesbian fiction.

"Continuing stories," she said. "An anthology of stories by great writers, only the stories don't exactly end at the end, see?" I nodded somewhat dubiously. "You know, they end with the words *to be continued* dot-dot-dot, and then there would be a second book the following season. The same authors continue their stories."

I had been around the publishing block enough times to know a great idea when I heard one. I wasted no time in offering to co-edit the book with Michele. And that, as they say, was the beginning of a beautiful friendship.

With Michele, I am pleased to present *To Be Continued...*, an anthology of page-turning, provocative writing by some of the hottest contemporary lesbian authors. In these pages you will find fantasy, romance, herstory, intrigue, and suspense. With humor, grace, and passion, the authors take you around the globe and through time, into worlds imagined and real. *To Be Continued...* will carry you to the edge and leave you hanging. Until the next time.

for my family,
biological and extended
MK

and for my family,
especially Terrie, Cookie, Harriet, and Charlie
KXT

CONTENTS

THREE WEDDINGS

LUCY JANE BLEDSOE

I. 1972

Marcia looked like a ghost coming down the aisle. She was no virgin, I should know, but she wore white satin with miles of lace just the same. Her skin was like skim milk, thin and bluish. Her father, by contrast, was radiant. Mr. Michaelson wore a black tux and walked ramrod straight, like Marcia was some great accomplishment of his. Actually, I have always believed she was. She got her big heart from him.

I wondered what Daddy would wear to my wedding, if I ever had one. All his buddies at the sanitation department would throw him a great party. I really couldn't imagine my getting married, but I hated the idea of depriving him of that. Maybe my being in law school made him even prouder than a wedding. Maybe.

By now I could see only the back of Marcia and I wished she was wearing jeans. All that flounce completely hid her ass. Her beautiful ass. I'd never said that to myself before. Oh, I'd said, and even to her, that Marcia was the most beautiful girl in the world. She is. And she has the biggest heart. Which she got in part from her father, rich and stiff as he was. But I'd never said to myself that I loved her ass.

As Marcia turned to face Jonathan at the altar, I said to myself, "What are you, Bonnie, some kind of dyke?"

Marcia and I met in English class our senior year in high school. She loved my poetry. It meant nothing to her that her father was a big shot attorney and my dad was a garbage collector. She wanted me to be a poet. Of all things! In the end, it was her father who wrote the letter that got me into law school. The Michaelsons are good people.

It was accidental that Marcia and I went to Cal together. By the time we became friends, we'd both already applied. We kissed for the first time on the day our acceptance letters came. Marcia was never afraid of touching. Nearly every Friday night we sat in her bedroom and I'd read her the poems I'd written that week and she'd stroke my hair. My muse was the anticipation of her hands. My poems elevated our relationship to something spiritual. On Friday nights after the poetry reading, when we lay on her floor in exaltation, Marcia would say, "This is religion," and I believed her.

Later, at Cal, Marcia even convinced her sorority to take me. But I drew the line there. I wasn't sorority material and I wasn't going to fake it. "We could share a room," Marcia begged. The idea of having Marcia every night of the week made my legs feel like giant amoebas. I just didn't have the nerve. Besides, I knew that those other bright, pony-tailed girls would smell us out. Marcia is so good-hearted. She doesn't see blood where I do.

I wore a pale blue polyester dress to the wedding. I got it at Penney's and it didn't fit very well, but I knew this would be the only time I'd wear it. I wasn't going to drop more than fifteen bucks for a one-time deal, period.

Listening to Marcia and Jonathan exchange vows was sort of

like doing acid. You just can't believe this other reality has been there all along and you'd missed it. Marcia had said to me, as recently as last week, "Don't you know you're the love of my life, Bonnie?" I had harrumphed. She'd grabbed both my ears, pulled me to her for a big kiss on the lips. We were downtown right at Union Square, too. My embarrassment only egged her on, and she kissed me again. That's when the tears came, the first and only time with Marcia.

"Bonnie," she'd said, trying to cup my cheeks in her hands, but I had pulled away, told her I was leaving and not to follow, and caught the subway home by myself. Twice since then she tried to talk about it, and I flat out refused.

Now the groom was kissing his bride. That's how the minister put it—"the groom may now kiss his bride"—and her voice echoed in my head. "No guy has ever kissed me like this." She told me that the first time, in her bedroom on the Friday night we got our acceptance letters. We kissed all night, and I came three times, just kissing.

I didn't look at Marcia when she glided back down the aisle with Jonathan, though I felt their wake. I glanced over and met eyes with Mr. Michaelson. He winked at me. I thought he felt the vacuum of that wake as fiercely as I did.

Driving to the country club for the reception, I worried about my wedding present. It didn't exist. In the trunk I had a box, wrapping paper, ribbon, tape, scissors, and a card. What did I think? There'd be a gift shop at the church? I pulled into a Long's Drugs, then left the parking lot without going in. Next I stopped at a Safeway, went in and walked the aisles, bought three oranges, and left. I sat in a parking space in front of a 7-11 for five minutes, eating one of the oranges, before driving away. Like there were going to be wedding gifts in those stores. Finally, I found a Walgreen's. An iron? A stuffed animal? A year's worth of office supplies? Scented soap? I left Walgreen's still wedding present-less.

I mingled at the reception, avoiding Jonathan's family. "Jonathan is from an old San Francisco family," Marcia had told me, like he was an antique worth millions. He probably *was* worth millions. Have you ever noticed how "old" is used as a euphemism for "rich"?

Jonathan himself, I have no feelings about. None. Although the only fight I've ever had with Marcia had to do with him. I told her, just once, and this was before the time I cried on Union Square, "I don't want you to marry this guy." She said, with an innocence I believe was sincere, "But Bonnie, why?"

"You love me," I answered, my heart slamming against my rib cage. I wonder now how it might have been different if I'd said, "Because I love you."

She stared at me for a long time, then said, "Yes, I love you. Of course I love you. But I still have to get married. What's the alternative?"

For her, it was a real question.

Normally, I would have been happy to shoot the breeze with either Marcia's dad or her mom, but although I'd been on excellent terms with them until a couple of months ago, things were a little rocky now. I almost flunked out of my first semester of law school when Marcia announced her engagement, which was an embarrassment to her father, who'd vouched for me. I wouldn't have gotten in if it weren't for the letter he'd written to the dean. "Almost flunked out" is not accurate. I did flunk out. But they gave me another chance and I did better the second semester, though hardly great. Then there was Marcia's mother, who was floored that I said no to being Marcia's maid of honor. Some honor. Mrs. Michaelson said, "Bonnie-honey"—I'm always "honey" or "dear" to them, though Marcia's other friends are called by their names—"don't be a bad sport." Then there was a flurry of comments about how "pretty" and "feminine" I'd look in the dress Marcia had picked. As if the problem were my needing reassurance about my femininity. Even my brother got in on the act, saying, "Get over it, Bon." Like he knew, or had just gotten it. Marcia's father was the kindest. He put his heavy hand on my shoulder and winked. I think he thought I was keeping my eye on the prize. In his generation, a woman chose between a career or womanly distractions, like weddings.

I could talk to Mr. Michaelson, I decided at the reception. He'd winked at me again, just a few minutes ago, behind Marcia and Jonathan moving swiftly up the aisle.

"Hello, Mr. Michaelson."

He threw an arm around my shoulders. "You sure look pretty," he said. I thanked him. Then he asked, "How's school?"

"Much better." I'd get straight A's from here on out I silently vowed. Mr. Michaelson was right: a woman had to make a choice.

As I chatted about the law with him, he and I both watched his daughter across the room, lightly holding onto Jonathan's arm. I wanted, more than anything in the world, to read Marcia a poem right then. To feel her fingers in my hair, knowing that later I would feel them everywhere. I knew there was a word for girls who wanted other girls, but that word didn't apply to me and Marcia. What we did was religion. I wondered what Mr. Michaelson was thinking.

The sugar bowl was crystal. Very pretty. I picked it up in full view of a couple dozen wedding guests and carried it high in front of my chest, as if it were slightly disgusting, away from the table. Anyone watching would presume I'd discovered ants crawling in the sugar, or maybe a glob of coffee-stained crystals. In fact, Mrs. Michaelson caught my eye and smiled gratefully. It was appropriate that I should quietly see to such matters.

I carried the sugar bowl into the ladies' room and dumped the sugar in the toilet. Then I washed the bowl in the sink and dried it with paper towels. Mrs. Michaelson would probably recognize it. She would tell her husband. One word from him to the dean and I'd be out of school.

The act was so childish, misguided, probably even ignorant, but I felt a need burning in my thighs, a need to disrupt, even the teeniest bit, this ancient ritual of privilege. The crystal sugar bowl traveled up my sleeve as I left the ladies' room. I went straight out to my car. There I wrapped it in the box, tied the bow real pretty, and took out the card.

To Marcia and Jonathan, I wrote. *From, The Alternative.*

II. 1982

Sarah Ann (pronounced "Saran," like the plastic wrap) and I had been fucking for three years. She was a free spirit, not a dyke, by her own description. Which made me nervous because she had "honesty spasms" during which she told people things as if she'd taken a truth serum. "Bonnie," she'd tell me, "my job is as much in jeopardy as yours, so you just don't have to worry about my blurting anything to anyone in the firm."

Good thing. I loved my job. I was making great money. I was very discreet. And about the free spirit part, well, that was okay, too. I didn't believe in labels. What I did with my body was my business. I'd come a long way since Marcia, but I'd never liked that word. Sure, I lusted after women. That basic appetite had always been with me, always would be. I just didn't see why everyone had to name everything.

Then Sarah Ann decided to get married. To some guy who had a boat in the marina down by Fort Mason. He lived on the boat—and so did she by the time of the wedding—and was "cool" according to Sarah Ann, which I think meant that he understood her "past." Which meant me. I'd become Sarah Ann's past.

Sarah Ann and I had awesome sex. She never quite wanted to "go to bed." That was too much of a commitment. So we did it in the dunes at Pt. Reyes, in the car after dark in the grocery store parking lot, once even in the supplies closet at work. I think she had the biggest orgasms of anyone I've known. She'd arch so hard her toes nearly kissed the back of her head, then she'd black out temporarily. I'd have to rock her for a few moments until she'd go, "Oh, oh, where am I?" Then she'd sigh long and deep and tell me, in great detail, what magical lands she'd just visited. Once I asked her, "Have you always come like this?" She looked away, which clued me immediately that these orgasms were not about me. Then she said, "At the center of my being is a universe of freedom. That's who I am, that's where my energy comes from." So I never made demands.

Imagine how shocked I was when Sarah Ann announced her engagement. Funny how fast a free spirit can evaporate when there's money, gifts, and family acceptance at stake. Sarah Ann's parents were overjoyed at her late marriage, and she began giving little speeches about how much she'd come to value her family. Like getting married gave her more family than me.

I never dressed dykey at the firm. I wore nice suits and usually diamond or pearl stud earrings. But when I received my wedding invitation in the mail, I knew instantly what I was going to do. I called Rosie and asked her if she'd be my date for a wedding. The invitation had not said, *Bonnie and Date,* but I ignored that. I hardly knew Rosie. We were in a professional women's group together. But I knew I could depend on her dressing right.

When I picked up Rosie, she was perfect. High femme. The silk fabric on her heels, which were a good two inches high, matched her silk dress perfectly, one of those tasteful muted colors that has no real name. Off-purple or purply-brown. I make it sound nauseating, but on her the color looked like nature, like her skin tone and the dress and shoes were put together by God. Elegant. I would have put money down that she'd be wearing a string of pearls and she was. Her earrings matched.

She smiled and took my arm as I led her to my Miata. I'd rented myself a tux. Spent three hundred dollars on it, made them alter everything so that it fit perfectly. "Who's getting married?" Rosie asked, squeezing my arm.

"Oh, an old girlfriend," I said tactlessly.

Rosie's smile foundered. "So we're showing her up, is that it?"

"Something like that," I said because I didn't know how to get my foot out of my mouth. And it wasn't exactly like I wanted to show up Sarah Ann. It was much bigger than that, but I couldn't yet articulate what I was feeling. In the car I smiled at Rosie, who was pretending to be looking for something in her purse as she decided just how big a shit I was. "Maybe we're showing me up," I told her. She gave me a sarcastic look, but seemed to reserve the possibility of finding out more interesting things about me nonetheless. I liked that. I like women who give you a couple of chances.

"I'd like you to meet my girlfriend," I said as I presented Rosie to partners from my firm. She played the part beautifully, graciously, taking all my cues. I saw the partners' wives eyeing her pearls and I figured they probably weren't real. That's the kind of thing lawyers' wives could tell. I took Rosie's hand and dragged her around, from food table to guest and back to food table. I eyed the dance floor when the band began, but Rosie whispered in my ear, "No, sweetheart."

I looked at her and she smiled at me, big like she really liked me.

"Are those pearls real?" I asked.

"You think I'm crazy? Why would I pay good money for real pearls when no one can tell the difference?"

"Good point," I agreed, adoring her for not knowing, in spite of her efforts as a member of my professional woman's group, that some women knew not only the difference but the shades of difference. And cared.

"What about that dress. Real silk?" I asked.

"What is this?" Rosie demanded. "Sure, it's real silk. Think I'm going to show up at a wedding in polyester?"

I smiled. "You look pretty."

"Good enough to make the bride squirm a little?"

"More than a little," I said. "Wanna meet her?"

"Sort of."

Sarah Ann wouldn't meet eyes with me as I introduced Rosie.

I couldn't tell if she was angry or hurt or mortified. But Rosie poured it on, saying, "I've heard so much about you from Bonnie." It was a total lie—I had never spent time with Rosie outside of meetings before. Sarah Ann flinched.

A few minutes later, I felt someone grab the material on the back of my tux and yank. It was Sarah Ann. "I'd like to talk to you," she hissed.

I followed her out to the parking lot. She wore a flowing pants outfit that went with her New Age wedding. "What are you doing?" she sneered, motioning to my tux.

Suddenly, I felt ashamed. I really hadn't meant to hurt her or to make a spectacle of myself at her wedding. "I guess I was just disappointed," I told her.

"Disappointed? Look, Bonnie, we never said—"

"Not about us. About weddings. There are all these values that come with marriage that are so deep they're transparent. People don't even see them. I've watched a lot of my friends get married and slam up against those values like metal on magnets. Wearing this tux makes me feel like I'm not a part of the false assumptions, that's all. This wedding feels very desolate to me, Sarah Ann. It's kind of like sending a love card that's already written and printed by the Hallmark company, rather than writing your own."

I'd never given a speech like that in my life and I felt lightheaded, like I was going to pass out.

"You're just jealous," she said. "I'd prefer it if you and that bimbo you brought left. Now."

"Okay," I said to her disappearing back. "We're gone."

I knew I couldn't get fired for wearing a tux to the wedding, but there were plenty of subtle things that could happen, like never making partner. Just the same, I was fine Monday morning, real fine. I wore my usual conservative pumps and suit, the very clothes Miss Free Spirit used to tease me about, but I felt like a different person. I sat down at my desk and picked up the phone, surprised to find it had the same heft, the same smooth plastic surface as always. I felt so different—lighter, even airy.

When I went to get coffee, I passed Mr. Roth, a senior partner, in the hall. Was that twinkle in his eye voyeuristic or respectful?

"Morning, sir," I said, as always.

"Great job on the Hadley's Hardware brief, Bonnie." He thudded me on the shoulder and passed by. Maybe he had a dyke daughter.

I felt excellent, just excellent. Back at my desk, I picked up the phone and made two calls. The first one was to the bride. I asked, "Would you like to fuck in the supplies closet at noon?" She hung up on me. Then I called Rosie and asked her out on a real date.

She said, "You mean because you'd like to see me and not just show up some ex?"

Sheepishly, I admitted, "You got it." I figured I could make it all up to her.

As I put the phone back in its cradle, I realized I'd just become a lesbian. In name as well as act. I liked the word. It was specific and concrete.

III. 1993

Ten years ago, Marcia left Jonathan and came out as a lesbian. Today she was celebrating her commitment to Carrie, who I thought was a lousy good-for-nothing two-timer, just another lover abusing Marcia's big heart.

The wedding was taking place on a grassy knoll on the edge of a cliff, overlooking the ocean. I stood at a distance for a long time, watching Marcia talk to some straight people who were acting oh so solemn, demonstrating their respect, their liberalness. That's why I hate gay or lesbian weddings. They feed the belief that queers are exactly like straight people except that we sleep with our own sex. Why not skip the wedding and just get on your knees and beg, "Oh, please, please. I'll mimic your every little move if you'll only accept me." Hell, half the reason I'm queer is to stay out of the ruts of tradition.

I eventually sidled up to Marcia, wedged myself between her and a straight woman, and whispered in her ear, "Come with me a minute, sweetheart?"

"What?" she asked, irritated.

"How about a quick kiss, over there in the bushes, for old times' sake. What do ya say?"

"Oh, for goodness sakes, Bonnie," she said. "Would you please—"

"Act right, for once?" I finished for her.

She pecked me on the cheek. "Go get something to eat."

The older Marcia got, the more she became her mother. Even if she had come out as a lesbian. I knew she loved me, but she couldn't help her eternal need to improve me.

I returned Marcia's peck, placing mine on her mouth, winked at the straight people, and ambled off. Food didn't sound so bad. Marcia usually was right about what I needed. At least I might get a meal out of this ordeal.

En route to the macrobiotic spread I saw Mrs. Michaelson, standing by herself, over in a grove of young fir trees. She looked perplexed as she waited for the ceremony to happen. Having perused the food table and found nothing edible-looking, I made my way through the wedding guests to her side.

"I was sorry to hear about Mr. Michaelson," I said, meaning it. It'd been a year since he died. I'd sent a note and all but hadn't seen Mrs. Michaelson in person since then.

"Thank you, Bonnie," she said.

He'd always been the one I'd liked most in the family, besides Marcia, of course. I didn't have much to say to Mrs. Michaelson. I glanced at her face, which was puckered in distaste. "You hate this wedding, don't you," I said.

"Hate it?" Mrs. Michaelson's laugh surprised me. "Oh, it just seems superfluous to me. Weddings."

I was shocked, her being a pillar of San Francisco's society and all. "What do you mean?" I asked.

She looked me in the eye and said, "You've always been such a straightforward woman, Bonnie. I wish Marcia had as much sense as you do."

"So do I," I agreed, looking over at Carrie, florid in her triumph over Marcia. That's what it was. Triumph. Marcia hadn't wanted this wedding. She'd been coerced into it. But what had brought on this flood of respect from Mrs. Michaelson?

She went on. "I'm seventy-two now. I don't regret my life, but I do regret all the shams. My marriage was one. I do believe the marriages of seventy-five percent of my friends are also shams."

Well, I'll be damned.

"When you get to be my age," Mrs. Michaelson continued, "you can say whatever you please."

"I started that real young," I commented.

"Come on," she said. "Let's take a quick walk before the ceremony."

"Excellent idea," I agreed, realizing that maybe I'd been as patronizing of Mrs. Michaelson as I had perceived her to be of me. I had no idea she had a free-thinking cell in her brain.

Mrs. Michaelson and I skidded down the red clay soil embankment in our dress sneakers—what do you wear to a beach wedding?—landing in the sand below.

"So much for my wedding outfit," I said, and she laughed. Besides my dress sneakers, I was wearing jeans and a T-shirt.

I stood, brushing myself off, and faced the sea. It was as if we were in a different world. No crepe paper, clicking cameras, forced smiles, people feeling their way timidly through rituals old and new. Thinking of the commitment ceremony made me want to shake myself hard, like a wet dog.

We walked along the beach, right next to the surf, and let the wind sprinkle us with sand. I glanced at Mrs. Michaelson, wondering what else she was thinking. She walked briskly, her face turned into the sunshine, smiling. Then, suddenly, she turned her smile on me. "So, Bonnie," she said, "there's not a piece of crystal for miles around. What will you wrap up for Marcia's gift? Shall we search the beach for a stone or shell?"

Mortification turned my legs to cement. Even as a big wave splashed up around my ankles, I stood still, squeezing my fists, looking at the sea foam sink into the sand at my feet. Finally, I said, "That's not funny."

"Oh, Bonnie—" she began in her overly sympathetic voice.

"No," I said. "I really don't think that's funny. How did you know? Did you know all along?"

"Dear, I saw you carry away the dish. Then it appeared in a package Marcia opened in front of all the guests after you'd left. How could I have not known?"

I felt very young, just as I did twenty years ago at that wedding. I turned toward the ocean. The sun, orange and hot, seemed to float on the horizon, then quickly it began sinking. It would be chilly soon.

"That really was priceless," Mrs. Michaelson chuckled.

"The sugar bowl?" I asked, overwhelmed with a fresh wave of guilt.

"No, what you did. It was the only bold stroke that whole day."

I squinted into the sun, realizing that she wasn't laughing at me. She was reveling in my mini-rebellion of some two decades ago. You just never knew where allies would come from.

"We'd better get back to the wedding," I said, slogging out of the surf.

"I suppose," she sighed. We walked back up the beach, then began climbing the embankment. I looked at Mrs. Michaelson as we reached the top, and she, too, was covered with the red clay soil.

"Oh, shit," I said, poking my head over the top. Folks were gathered around the food table, filling their plates with tofu dip, veggie pilaf, and about eighty-five different kinds of bean dishes. "It's over. We missed the ceremony."

Heads turned as one of the brides' mothers and first girlfriend emerged over the embankment, covered in red mud. I got to my feet first and lent a hand to Mrs. Michaelson. She took it, but couldn't get a grip because it was slick with the clay soil. I wiped my hand on my jeans and reached out to her again. This time I pulled her over the top of the bank and all the way to her feet. She laughed, and so did I.

"I'm hungry," Mrs. Michaelson said, ignoring the wedding guests who stared at us. "Let's get something to eat."

I followed her, holding my head up like the aristocrat she was and I wasn't, and filled my plate with vegetarian morsels. After all that wind and sea and soil I sure could have used a steak. Then we carried our plates and sat back down on the edge of the cliff and let our feet dangle.

I knew the footsteps were Marcia's. I looked over my shoulder and saw her in her lavender silk jumpsuit, walking toward us, glaring.

TO BE CONTINUED...

ROAD MAPS

NISA DONNELLY

GAS * F OD * GAS

O U R I S T   C A B I N S

FRIED RIVER CATS

C O D B E E R

MECHANIC ON CALL

JERSEY STATION 3 MI ES

KRIS & SHELLY, 1992

What do you suppose fried river cats are?"

"Obviously something that goes with cod beer. As in, 'Give me two cod beers and a fried river cat to go.'"

We've been driving too long, I decide, watching trees taller than any I remember seeing march along the side of the two-lane highway. We have tumbled into a tunnel of green, splotches of sun glint over my right shoulder. Kris lights another cigarette (she'd promised me she would quit smoking after this trip), looks over at me, and winks. *How's it going, kiddo?* I blink and smile. Fine. Two days ago we stopped talking about why we're here, or even where we're going. Now, we're reduced to bad jokes and communicating through winks and smiles. We're running from the past. Like convicts, it doesn't matter so much where we go, just as long as we keep on going and never stop to look back.

Not that there's much to look back on. Her husband, my mother. Ex-husband, she would correct, although they aren't officially divorced. She plans to take care of that once we get to where we're going, soon as we decide where we're going. "It's not as if we have kids or nothing," she said the first day out, when I could still smell New Jersey in the air. "It's not as if your mom couldn't expect you to go. Hell, she won't even miss you. She's got that new guy...what's his name? Harley?" "Harry." "Right, Harry."

I met her on the night shift at the SHOP 'N SAV, where I was the assistant night manager. She used to come in to buy cigarettes and beer. "You shouldn't smoke." Those were the first words I said to her. She pulled her sunglasses down lower on her nose — sunglasses even though it was nearly midnight — and looked at me closely. "And why is that...Shelly?" She read my nametag, then looked up at me and grinned. I felt the color rise until my cheeks burned. "Because...I mean...it's not good for you."

"It's not good for you, *Kris.*"

"What?"

"Kris, that's my name. Kris Monroe." The way she said it, *mun-row-a,* made me smile. "And what are you, a medical student or something?" She was teasing, maybe flirting, although I couldn't imagine why. I felt the color coming again. "You blush, I like that." She winked at me and then she was gone.

I watched her through the window: how she carried the beer in one hand, opened the door of an old red pickup with the other; how easily she swung in, lit a cigarette, gunned the engine. An old man pulled into her space, blocking my view of which way she turned. The next night she was back. And the night after that. One night she bought a lottery ticket and won two dollars. "You're good luck, Shelly. What time do you get off?" We sat out in the parking lot drinking beer, talking, watching the sun come up. She was married, she told me, to a boy she'd dated in high school. They were better friends than lovers. He owned a piece of his brother's gas station across town. She wasn't happy and didn't know why. I told her about Mama, and how I'd just finished my second year at junior college studying business management, and how I was in line for a promotion at the SHOP 'N SAV—day manager—as soon as there was an opening. When she drove me home, she touched my arm and said, "Can I see you again?"

That was how it started. And now here we were, on a highway somewhere in Kentucky, following a river road, heading in the general direction of California. But if some place better caught our fancy along the way, we could stay there, too. That was our plan. "So long as the cash and the credit cards hold out," she'd said. She'd taken eight thousand dollars from their joint savings account, leaving him with four hundred and change and the furniture, and I had my last two paychecks, still uncashed, in my purse. We'd do okay. As long as we didn't look back.

"So, you up for some cod beer and fried river cats?" she's asking. The sign, the same one we'd seen three miles back, but in slightly better shape, now has an arrow attached and is pointing toward a blacktop.

"What do you suppose fried river cats really are?"

"I think you'll know soon enough, Shelly. The engine's running hot again, and according to that sign there's a mechanic on call."

I stare at the blacktop road leading to our right, then at the weathered sign. It doesn't look promising, but the map says there's nothing else for a good twenty miles. "I just hope the mechanic's in better shape than his sign."

Kris shrugs and turns onto the blacktop. "Well, pardner, I reckon we're about to find out."

"I reckon we are."

DEVIL'S LANDING

The Devil's Landing marks the juncture of three great rivers: the Wabash, the Ohio, and the mighty Mississippi. No one knows what the first residents of this land called it. Not a one of them survives, and those who came later couldn't have understood their language even if there had been a trace of it left, so skillful was the uprooting and displacement of the original inhabitants by the traitors who followed. And those who followed didn't name this place Great Rivers or Three Rivers or even Mighty Rivers, all of which might have made some sense. No, the first of the land pirates who floated down the Ohio to this point was struck dumb with homesickness and named the perilous sandbars that greeted him Jersey, imagining the place looked more like the England he'd left than it actually did. There are photographs and etchings enough to prove that.

And Jersey it remained. Not that it mattered much; so little was there that few stopped, unless it was to pitch a rangy tent overnight, and none stayed. The sprawling cluster of homesick vagrants who'd originally given the spot its name had long since moved on or died. Inhospitable as it was—blisteringly hot in summer, rampant with plague-bearing mosquitoes, or damp and frozen in winter, subject to floods and the rude appearance of sandbars that seemed to grow of their own volition—Jersey attracted none of the more affluent, which is to say upstanding, settlers who were building homes in the towns that had begun to spot the riverbank. It did, however, attract the attention of a few unlucky, hardscrabble Danish farm families who had unfortunately pooled their inheritances, savings, and children's futures to buy, sight unseen, one thousand forty-seven acres of riverfront farmland known as Jersey Station.

They brought with them seventeen starving Irish (ten men, four women, and three boy children) they'd picked up at the docks in New York. Three Wesley Methodist missionaries who (wrongly) believed there were heathens there awaiting conversion and a mission trailed along behind, looking for souls to convert. The Wesley Methodists were reportedly disappointed in finding none of the original inhabitants still in residence, but did welcome the opportunity to convert the heathen Irish, who were Catholics and therefore almost as good as bona fide heathens, if considerably less exotic than the unintelligible Danes, who, even though they didn't speak the language, still managed to comprehend that they and the missionaries all had deeds to the same one thousand forty-seven acres of land presently inhabited by four renegade slaves, a family of Portuguese fishermen, and three Croats who spent their winters trapping beaver and the rest of the year digging coal out of holes no wider than a mule's hindquarters.

As far as anyone knows, they settled in with a kind of uneasy peace. The ex-slaves spoke to no one. The Portuguese aligned themselves with the Danes, although neither could understand the other's language nor the language of the world they now inhabited. The Croats and the Irish, bonded apparently by God if not the blessed Virgin, spent Sundays together in a clearing near the largest stand of oaks and made plans to build a church. The missionaries did the same, only considerably closer to the river, since Wesley Methodists had a strong need for river immersions during the baptismal ceremonies. No one was sure if the Catholics didn't have a need for river water, or if they simply wanted to worship as far removed from the Wesley Methodists as possible. Or maybe they just liked trees. One year passed, then two, finally ten. The churches, such as they were, had been built. And the houses. Gardens were tended. Crops planted. Children born and fish caught. The women birthed each other's babies and the men helped each other in the fields. They had drawn their lines of familiarity and opposition, supported each other when they had to and killed each other when they had to. They kept to themselves and belonged to each other.

And then, it began to rain.

The little log church by the river was the first to be washed away. The Catholics congratulated themselves on having had the good sense to build further inland. Everyone began counting days, unsure what they actually would do if it again rained forty days and forty nights and equally unsure if they should start counting over if it stopped raining and then started again. The river kept rising, splashing against the sides of the log houses, carrying away seed and livestock, chickens, two children—one Irish, one Danish—and the oldest of the Croat trappers. The Catholic church was the last to go. By then, the people, most of them, were gone. Those who hadn't headed north or west had been swallowed by the river or had died from the typhus that it carried. By the time the Confederate Army arrived in one of its secret night raids, so little was left that even they moved on, weary of mud and rotted dreams.

The river washed up and over Jersey all that spring and for half the summer. Boats were lured into its shallows and treacherous sandbars. Ghosts were said to inhabit the woods that surrounded what was left of the village. The ex-slaves, who had found their way to Cairo, which was not so far away and its own promised land of a sort, reported what had happened. The fires, the sickness, the river rising and rising and showing no mercy. And they hadn't stayed to the very end, at that. Who knows what evil really happened there, at the Devil's Landing?

So it became the Devil's Landing. And here is where this story begins, in 1888, when a dandy wearing diamond rings and diamond studs got up from a card game in Philadelphia, tucked a deed into the inside pocket of his jacket, tipped his hat to the dregs at the table, checked his watch, and walked into the morning. Eight months later, he waded through the muck and climbed the mud bank, making his way to the oversized log house, where oiled paper was rolled up to let in a bit of April breeze. He stopped at the door, checked his gold watch, lit a cigar, and stepped into the dark and musty room. Two fishermen were hunkered over glasses of cheap whiskey. They raised rheumy eyes to survey the dandy in their midst. A woman rose from the dusk of a far corner and made her way across the room. Bare feet. She grinned, turned to the men at the table. "Well, lookie what we got here." The men at the table grunted. The dandy's cigar glowed orange. "River washed us up a city boy. What you doin' here, city boy?"

"Just come to claim what's mine," the dandy said, studying the cigar, not even glancing in the woman's face.

"Come to claim what's his'n," she said, dragging out the words, shaking her hips a little, side to side. One of the fishermen at the table sniffed, wiped his finger under his nose, then grinned. Toothless. "Well, shows what he knows, I'd say. Shows he don't even know where he is."

"Oh, I know, all right."

"This here is Devil's Landing," the other fisherman said. "Everybody round here knows if it belongs to any man, it belongs to the devil hisself."

"Then," said the dandy, "I must be the devil, because I have the deed to this place and damned near everything else you can see from here. Now, I'd like a drink. Brandy if you have it, whiskey if you don't. And forget the glass, the bottle looks safer."

The woman laughed, picked up the bottle off the table where the fishermen were sitting, and extended it, bottom first. "What'd you say your name was?"

"I thought you heard," he said, taking a drink, then looking her full in the eye for the first time. "The Devil."

WANDALEE 1925-1993

Where you girls say you was from? New Jersey. Is that right?

Well, I guess the name of this place is what made you curious, right? Course, I got to tell you, nobody calls it Jersey Station, 'cept on the maps. That's why we put it on the sign. Ever'body 'round here still calls it Devil's Landing, or just the landing. You come up along this way and ask for the landing and they'll direct you here, 'specially if you say you're looking for Wandalee at the landing. Been here all my life. Mazie's been here most of hers. She's off in the big house having her nap. She'll be down after a while, take a look at your engine. What'd you say you thought the matter was? Well, don't matter, wouldn't mean nothing to me. Mazie's the one who knows her way around an automobile. We got a deal—I don't mess with her garage, she don't mess with my bar.

You probably noticed they's not a lot here now. Don't have to be a genius to know that. But you got to look past what it is and into what it was. And, oh, let me tell you, it was something in its time. Jersey. Doesn't have a thing to do with that place back East, New Jersey, although them that's fond of history sometimes thinks that. Or cows, although that would be more likely. Of course, I can't really say how it come by its name for sure, but I can tell you about the Devil. He was a powerful force around here. In fact, there's them that say Jersey Station always belonged to the Devil. And they'd be right. The Devil finally come back to claim his due, and everything here was his. Even us. We ain't nothing much, but are all the Devil's kin.

Six streets, every one of them dead-ending on the Mississippi River. When I was comin' up it was a real town, not like now. We had a post office, two restaurants that served up catfish could make a grown man cry, three taverns, a Standard Oil station, a boat repair and body shop, more'n thirty houses, two churches, a town hall, the dry goods store, a grocery, and a couple bait-and-tackle shops, and the hotel with the deck that looked out over the river. That burned down, oh, sometime during the war. Wasn't no reason to rebuild it. No call for three-story hotels.

So my sister and her husband Dak, they was runnin' the hotel at the time, took the insurance money and put up the motel. That must've been in, oh, 1948, '49. Just a year or so before Dak run off. Sissy didn't last more'n a couple years after that. I said, "Ain't no man worth dryin' up over," but she always was the sensitive one. Like when all her babies was born with something bad wrong with 'em. Well, she like to never get over that and didn't have the sense enough to tell Dak no more, if you know what I mean. So it wasn't no surprise to me that all that misery just built up and grew a tumor in her brain. He tried coming back for the funeral, but Mazie and I wouldn't have none of it.

Oh, now Mazie was quite a card in them days. We'd just met. I was running the motel for Sissy, 'cause she was sick even then, when I heard this horn honking outside. There was Mazie, behind the wheel of a black Cadillac. They stopped making them during the war, you know, so this wasn't all that new, but it was shiny as an obsidian mirror. She was grinning, I remember that. And I thought, Lord have mercy, that big woman don't have sense enough to see this ain't no drive-in. I got to the passenger side and was set to tell her that I wasn't no carhop, when she rolled down the window. That's when I seen all these handles around the steering wheel. Next thing I noticed was that she didn't have but the one leg. The right one was cut off clean above the knee. Come to find out that had happened during the war— she wasn't fighting, of course, it got caught in some machinery in one of the ship-building plants out by San Francisco. They gave her thirty-five thousand dollars 'cause she wasn't but twenty years old when it happened.

Mazie has what you might call a natural affinity for engines. She just puts her ear next to one and can tell you in about twenty seconds what the problem may be. Then, if she likes you well enough, she'll fix 'er for you. If she don't, well she'll at least give you the dime to call in the tow truck. You say your vehicle is overheating? Well, you come to the right place. After Mazie gets up from her nap, we'll have her come on out and give it a listen. Her people were from down by the Texas border, where it's so danged hot, you either take a nap of an afternoon or you die wishin' you had. It's a habit she come by natural. Not like she's lazy or anything like that, no indeed. Me, now I never could get into the habit of sleeping while the sun was still high. I do my work sunup to sunset, the way the Lord willed it. Mazie, though, she's a night person. Likes to be up late. Some nights she stays up so late, our paths don't cross until lunchtime. But that's fine by me, I've got my own work to tend to. And so does she, for that matter.

Anyway, she never let that leg or the lack thereof get in her way. Mazie said she'd been driving across the country and had an idea that she wanted to get in some fishing. Catfish. I said, "Hell, you come to the right place." So she moved into cabin number five, 'cause it's right next to the path down to the boat dock— not so far for her to walk, you see. She stayed there, oh, for six months, maybe eight, before the floods came and she moved into the big house with me. It was Mazie's idea to add on the post office and the grocery store and the bait-and-tackle, and when the Standard Oil station closed down, she had the Mobil people bring out a couple of pumps, so we got that, too. Course, bring-ing in the restaurant and the bar was my idea. Now we're pretty much all there is. Except for the boat repair and body shop— Mazie don't do no body work. And the church, of course. The minister don't live here in town, though. We share with a couple little churches on up the highway. That's how it gets to be. First the young people take off, and then there ain't nobody left but a bunch of withered-up old river rats like us.

And that big brick building you passed on the blacktop? That was the school—grade, middle, and high. The county closed it down more'n twenty years ago. Started busing the youngsters to one they built about eight miles east on the highway. It's a yel-low concrete block affair, with air conditioners. Looks a lot like the pictures I've seen of prisons, which is not to say I've ever actually seen a prison myself. But I keep up. At three o'clock ev-ery afternoon I tune in to *A Current Affair*. Let me tell you, the world ain't what it used to be. I been watching that program ever since they come three years back when we was having the floods.

Course, the floods ain't nothing to us. Hell, we been living underwater half the year ever since the levee got put up on the wrong side of town. See, instead of it running along next to the river like you'd expect, with the houses and so forth on the other side, ours is a bit different. The federal government wanted to buy us out, the whole town. Said the floods was costing too much. Didn't offer us nothing but spit and air and promises, and no way what this town is worth. Wanted to come in, doze us down. So that's how we ended up on *A Current Affair.* 'Cause of the protest and all. In the end, we didn't have to sell out. Still don't have no flood insurance, though. Hell, we just do like we always did: wait for the water to come on in and then get out the hip waders and the boats. It only happens once, maybe twice, ever couple years or so. Don't last long. Least not long enough to lose your whole town over.

You want some of that berry pie? I made it myself this mornin'. I do like a good raspberry pie. Course, Mazie, she don't much care for it. Says them little seeds get stuck under her partial. Well, I got my own teeth, I tell her, and if I've gotta hunger for berry pie, then berry pie it is. No, no, you don't owe me nothin'. Like my granddaddy, I charge for the beer and the whiskey; the pie's on the house.

Just about everyone hereabouts has their own version as to how the levee ended up on the wrong side of town. Some say it never would've happened if Al Capone hadn't developed a fondness for fishing back in 1922. Or if he hadn't taken a fancy to the Devil. Now there is an equally small contingent what credits it to Amos Marion, the county land assayer who was known to have come back from World War I with a morphine habit, generously supplemented with his best friend and lifelong companion Jim Beam. The more reasonable think it was just poor planning by the Jersey Station Town Council. But they all agree it comes back to the Devil, which is to say my grandfather. Now, you got to remember times was different then. The Devil was a whiskey runner in those days. It was the only way he could figure to keep his speak supplied. Well, course it wasn't so much a speak as a barge he just parked out there in the middle of the river. He'd ferry folks back and forth. Oh, there was good times on that boat. Not that I remember all that much, I was just a little runt then...wouldn't't've guessed it to look at me now, would you? But it was true. You see this ring? More'n a full-carat diamond. Mazie's got the other one. I give it to her, oh, some time back. They was both the Devil's. He was a man did like fine things.

When the Devil passed on, it was back in 1940, he was old, but well kept. A full head of hair, white and thick as anything you ever seen. Wore his diamond rings right up to the end, diamond studs, too, although he wasn't buried with them neither. No way. The Devil was too practical for that. Always had a taste for fine whiskey and redheaded women. My grandmomma, who died when my own momma was just a little bitty thing, had the reddest hair. We buried him with his hands crossed over her picture just like he wanted. We did everything just like he wanted. Didn't pay not to. And I mean that in the very literal sense.

See, the Devil was rich. Came from a family with money someplace back East. The Devil never spoke their name, least not so I ever heard. Said they'd paid him off to leave, gave him ten thousand dollars and said there'd be another ten thousand waiting for him out in San Francisco when he got there. This would've been back around the turn of the century, I suppose. Well, he took that ten thousand dollars and got on a boat that sailed all the way down one side of South America and up the other. Took him three years. Gambling and whoring and drinking whiskey all the way. By the time he hit San Francisco, that ten thousand dollars had turned over a half dozen times, but there was still that other ten thousand waiting. By the time he was done a year later, he had twelve times that amount and the deed to twenty-five hundred acres of bottom land along the Mississippi that he won off some poor sonofabitch who didn't know you can't never beat a professional gambler.

The Devil asked my grandmother—truth be told, she was a working girl who'd had the misfortune to find herself in the family way—if she wanted to go on a riverboat ride. Apparently she didn't have a whole lot of better offers. And like I said, he did have a fondness for redheaded women. My momma was born on a riverboat tied up at the Jersey Station dock. Said she tried to wait but was so excited to see this town her daddy owned that she couldn't, and the sight was such that it struck her blind. She thought that was funny, my momma. She had what you'd call an odd sense of humor. You don't expect that in a blind woman. And she was pretty, too. Redheaded like her mother, with skin that was so pale you could almost see her veins. Sissy looked like her. I'll show you their picture later. Me, I ended up looking like Papa. Fortunately, though, the resemblance stopped there.

My father was a sour man. I honestly believe he blamed the world for *him* being blind, and he took it out on my poor mother and Sissy. And me, although I was considerably harder to catch. I learned my way around him when I was first getting land legs. It's not as easy as you might think. See, my father was a genius. I'm not saying that because he was my father. Everybody said so. Even Harvard College said so. Of course, being a genius didn't make up for him being blind. In the end, there wasn't a university in all of Boston—that's where his people were from—that wanted to have anything to do with a blind history professor. Nor in New York City. Or Atlanta. Or Washington, D.C. He tried them all. Got on a train and went from one college to the next. Not a one of them would have him. People were ignorant in those days.

When he was making the rounds in Chicago, he heard about a little bitty nothing of a college about a hundred miles from here that had a program just for blind students. They hired him. Who wouldn't? A bona fide genius, a Harvard education to match, and blind in the bargain. The people at that college must've thought it was their lucky day.

My father wasn't born blind, you see. He'd been able to see just as well as you or me up until he was about twenty-five years old. He told me once it was as if somebody kept turning the lights down a little bit at a time. It came on so slowly that he didn't really notice until it was too late. Not for the doctors, they couldn't have done anything about it in those days, but for him. I think he regretted not paying better attention all those years.

He used to ask me, "Girl, what color is that flower I smell?" It would be the lilac bush, or maybe the tuberose. And I'd say, "Purple or pink," whatever it was, you know. And he'd say, "No, what color is it?" And I'd have to describe every detail to him, the shape of every petal, the way the sun shone on each blossom, the drops of morning dew, the way a lady spider was spinning her web. He made me pay attention, to look at things hard, to really see them. Mazie says that's what she likes about me, the way I really see things. You'd be surprised at how many people just shuffle through life never taking the time to really see anything. My papa was a blind man, but he taught me to see the details of life. Lots of men with twenty-twenty vision don't do as much for their daughters.

He met Momma at that college where he was the history professor. She pretended to have a deep and abiding interest in history, but actually it was the teacher with the baritone voice that grabbed her fancy. She took every class he taught. History of Civilization I and II, the War Between the States, the History of British Conflict, and the Revolutionary War, Parts I and II. By the time they got to the Revolutionary War, Part III, she and Daddy were engaged. They were married just two days after graduation, three days after her final examination in History of the American West. She got a B. Momma said it was because Daddy didn't want the other students to think that he played favorites. Daddy said it was because she, after snaring the professor, let her studies go and deserved a B. They fought about that B for as long as I can remember. May be fighting about it still, if you can carry a grudge into the hereafter.

He stayed on to teach another year after they were married, even though the Devil was after them all the time to come back home. Sending Momma off to college was one thing, her staying gone was like a slap in my grandfather's face. It got worse after she had Sissy.

The Devil would drive down to that college town—what a sight that must've been. Big white Cadillac convertible with the Devil behind the wheel and whichever woman he'd taken up with at the time cuddled up next to him. Winter or summer, the top down. Honking the horn from the time he turned into the college grounds until my father came out of whatever classroom he was teaching in. Of course, I wasn't around to see it, but I heard the story often enough. Daddy would come out of the history building, his white cane *tap-tapping* in front of him, his collar buttoned tight. "Sir, we are trying to educate young minds here. If you don't mind."

But the Devil did mind, of course. That was the whole point.

Finally, when Momma was carrying me and Daddy's health was starting to fail—did I mention that he'd had diabetes since he was a boy, which is why he was blind—the Devil finally got his way. They came back here. Daddy brought forty-seven wooden crates of history books, most of them in braille. Momma brought Sissy, who was walking by then, and me who was still giving her gas when she lay wrong at night, but not for much longer. The Devil set them up in the big house and moved into the hotel with my sixth grandmother, a redheaded woman named Deidre who had come down from Chicago. All my grandmothers either came down from Chicago or over from St. Louis or up from Memphis. Like I said, the Devil's taste in women was fairly specific.

Deidre is the grandmomma I remember. I got a picture of her and the Devil on their wedding day here somewhere. Deidre didn't have much of a lap as I recall, but I loved her voice, deep and husky. I don't think I ever saw her without a package of Pall

Malls stuck under her bra strap. She's the one who taught me how to fry catfish. On the whole, Deidre wasn't what you'd call a fine cook. Her pies were too sweet, her gravy too stiff, her mashed potatoes too runny. And she believed in boiling her vegetables until they turned this peculiar shade of gray, like something washed up on the shore. But that woman could turn a catfish until it was crispy gold on the outside and white and flaky inside.

She's the one who talked the Devil into opening up the kitchen in the hotel. People from all over would come just to eat her catfish and drink beer. Of course, this was during Prohibition, so I suppose they were really coming for the beer and the catfish was just a cover. No matter. On Friday nights there'd be folks three and four deep on that balcony that overlooked the river, eating catfish and waiting for the johnboat that would take them on out to the barge. That's where the real action was. The Devil had bought himself a barge and turned it into a regular floating casino. Out there on the water you could get anything you wanted. Scotch. Gin. Canadian whiskey. The Devil had connections. And there was always a band on weekends. Oh, it was a party that never stopped, and when they were tired from gambling and drinking, the Devil would haul 'em back across the water to the hotel where Deidre had a clean bed and a friendly woman waiting for them if that was their taste. So long as they still had a buck in their pocket, the Devil was their friend.

The Devil took care of us. And the state police and the county sheriff and even a few of the Army Corps of Engineers and the Coast Guard. Thanks to all those Prohibition party nights, we all rested well during the tough years that followed. My sister and I grew up during the Depression, but we didn't know hardly nothing about that.

See that picture over the bar? That's Deidre. She's a looker, ain't she? Not like any kinda grandmomma you ever seen, I'd reckon. Some outta work artist that the Devil met up with in Chicago come and painted that. Stayed in room number three, up at the top of the stairs. Never had no interest in the girls, which was just fine with Deidre, because she wasn't opposed to givin' out a clean bed in exchange for something fine, like a painting or what have you, but she wasn't sure her girls was of the same mind. He wanted to paint fish. Can you imagine that? Fish. Well, he did do some of that. Saw one of his fish pictures in a magazine once. Just looked like your common old river cat to me, but must've been something special 'cause that picture ended up in the natural history museum. But you can't paint fish in the winter, so he painted Deidre and the girls. The Devil wasn't about to sit still for a portrait. I always did think Deidre had him sort of enhance...you know, her upstairs regions...'cause I don't quite remember all that bein' there.

Liked to killed her when the Devil passed. She laid up in the big house wailing. I've been at birthings that was more quiet. You could hear her all over the town. Momma said it was 'cause she was full-blooded Irish and they do like that when they're grief-stricken. I personally thought she was going mad. Maybe she was. But she was the one who wouldn't let none of the undertakers around here take care of the Devil. Sent for an undertaker all the way from St. Louis. Stayed in the room while the man did his duty. Wouldn't let nobody touch the Devil, except for my pa, without her being there. Everybody thought that was right strange, because there never was all that much love lost between my pa and his father-in-law, you understand. "I made your grandpa a promise" was all he'd say when I asked why he took such an interest in the funeral.

Do you know I was a grown woman before I knew the truth? More'n thirty years old. And then only because the old man was gone senile. It was Decoration Day the last year he was alive, and I took him up to the cemetery to Momma's grave and Sissy's. Me and Mazie used to like to take him up there, but later on, the walk got to be too much for her, the ground so rough and all. We were walking along, me describing the colors to him, and we came to the Devil's marker. It's an angel made out of black marble with folded arms and drooping wings. Deidre had it carved special after a picture she found in a magazine. I guess she thought the Devil would like it, but the thing personally gives me the creeps. See, she didn't want it to be looking at her into eternity, so she had the stonecutter keep its eyes closed but its mouth open—she figured angels would like to sing. I was telling Pa how the wild roses I set out around all the graves have taken to spreading, even over to the Devil's grave. And the Devil wasn't one who ever had a fondness for roses, or flowers of any sort so far as I know.

"Odd woman," my pa said. "Thought nobody knew." I figured he was talking about Deidre. I said how she wasn't no more or less odd than anybody else. Besides, she'd stuck with the Devil right up till the end, and that should have amounted to some kind of gratitude on our part, 'cause he wouldn't have none of us take care of him. And Papa laughed. Not a big laugh, like something was truly funny, but sort of a series of little huffs. "You don't know nothing!" He was starting toward my mother's grave. "I thought you would be the one who would know, but you never did figure it out. I said, 'You can't fool me. I may be blind, but you can't fool me.' Everybody has their price, Wandalee. And then I thought what difference does it make? The Devil had me, bought and paid for the minute we moved into his town, so what difference did it make if I knew the Devil was a...female? Who was I going to tell? So I didn't. I told God. But I don't think God ever listened to me. Wandalee, what color did you say the wild roses are? You must pay attention to details. Very important. Very important to take it all in. Very important...to know."

Let me go call Mazie. She won't want to miss *A Current Affair*, and if she's gotta do some work on your truck, that might take some time. Course, you girls are welcome to stay the night. We got tourist cabins. Real nice. Twelve bucks, and that includes breakfast. Hell, you ain't going to find nothing better between here and...well, I can't think of nothing better period. Not for that price. You want to do some fishing, we got boats. I could let you have one for...oh, how's three bucks sound? And bait. You like to fish? I never used to care for it all that much, but Mazie likes it and damned if I didn't find my way to likin' it, too. Course, my river cats is net-caught. Ralph brings 'em by of an evening. He'll be along directly. Tell you what I can do. Twenty bucks and I'll give you the boat and a cabin and dinner. Fried catfish and all the beer you can drink. You ain't in a hurry to get nowhere are you? No, I didn't think so. Anyway, here's the key to number five. You go on over there, and I'll call Mazie. Tell her we got company for supper and she's got a engine to listen to. And I'm gonna find that wedding picture of the Devil and Miss Deidre for you. Think you might like to have a look at that while you're here.

Number five turned out to be a small, white clapboard cabin in a clearing next to a gravel driveway behind Wandalee's bar. Like the exterior, the walls were white as were the floors. From the smell, it was freshly painted. Yellow-and-white checked curtains hung at the windows, which Kris opened. We could smell the river and hear it, but the trees blocked our view. Over the bed hung a painting of another reclining nude, possibly one of Deidre's "girls," a tall, bronze woman with huge hands and full lips. The bed was covered with a quilt, obviously old, handmade and worth a fortune in the city. How did Wandalee keep her guests from stealing? Or maybe there never were any other guests.

"Do you think she's nuts, Kris? I mean what if there isn't a Mazie and we've ended up...or what if there is and she's nuts, too?"

Kris flopped down on the bed, stretching like a cat. "God, I think I've died and gone to heaven. This is a feather mattress."

"But what if she's...you know...nuts?"

"At twenty bucks a night and all we can eat, she can be as nuts as peanut brittle for all I care. Besides, she's an old woman, what's she gonna do? Sick the Devil on us? Hell, some cross-dressing old dyke. Besides, I think she's interesting. Come on, babe, we said we were looking for adventure, see America, all that crap.

It'll give us something to tell our grandchildren."

Kris was smiling, talking more to herself than to me, the way she does when she's falling asleep. I sat on the edge of the bed, stroking her back. She was right. Wandalee seemed harmless enough, just old and lonely. Mazie's probably just like her. The sound of the river *lap-lapping* against its bank began to wash through me. Just a little nap, I thought, stretching out next to Kris, who was already snoring softly.

Closing my eyes, I tried to picture Wandalee and Mazie in this cabin. Had they fallen in love or just fallen in together somehow, the way some couples seem to? And what about the Devil and the beautiful Deidre? What must that have been like? In the distance, I could hear music and laughter. A party. Footsteps on the gravel driveway. Boat oars in water. Ghosts dancing on their barge. The Devil dressed in diamond rings and diamond studs, ferrying people back and forth across the water, laughing, while Deidre waited on shore.

TO BE CONTINUED...

JOE LOUIS WAS A HECK OF A FIGHTER

JEWELLE GOMEZ

Gilda was more than alive. The 150 years she carried were flung casually around her shoulders, an intricately knit shawl handed down from previous generations, yet distinctly her own. Her legs were smooth and mocha brown, unscarred by the knife-edge years spent on a Mississippi plantation, and strengthened by more recent nights dancing in speakeasies and discos. The paradox did not escape Gilda: her power was forged by deprivation and decadence, and the preternatural endurance that had been thrust upon her unexpectedly. Her grip could snap bone and bend metal, and when she ran she was the wind, she was invincible and alone.

Tonight, hurrying toward home to Effie, she walked anxiously, gazing at the evening skyline. It sparkled like Effie's favorite necklace, which plunged liquid silver between her dark breasts. The image pushed Gilda faster through the tree-shrouded park. She glanced over her shoulder at the shadowed sidewalk behind her, where the light from the streetlamps was cast through shifting leaves. Little moved on the Manhattan avenue at this late hour, but Gilda knew danger was not far behind her.

Gilda had not seen any of her siblings since she'd escaped slavery more than one hundred years before. Their loss was so remote, Gilda was always surprised when an image of them arose in her mind. It was the same with Samuel. Not a relative, but a blood relation, Samuel's face had haunted her path since they'd met in Yerba Buena just before the turn of the century. The town had been exploding with prosperity, much like New York was now. Gold almost coursed down the hills into the pockets of seamen, traders, bankers, and speculators, until its pursuit became a contagion.

Gilda easily remembered her first impressions when she'd met Samuel: greed, selfishness, fear. That volatile blend had swirled through Samuel's eyes like mist from the Bay. Even when he'd smiled, Gilda knew he despised her. Seeing him again tonight had left Gilda feeling chilled and sluggish. She continued walking, slowly turning over in her mind every word he'd said, trying not to let the surprise of his appearance alarm her. When he'd stepped from the doorway on upper Broadway Gilda had been preoccupied with getting home. Samuel had appeared abruptly in front of her, giving an elaborate bow as if it were still 1890.

"The not-so-fair Gilda lives, I see," Samuel had intoned, the taut agitation of his voice unchanged after almost one hundred years.

"Samuel," Gilda answered simply, as if she were greeting him in one of the Yerba Buena salons they used to frequent. She said no more but shifted her weight in preparation for his attack.

"Gilda, why so pugnacious? I'm only looking up an old friend."

"What do you want, Samuel?"

"I've just stated my intention. One would think you'd be more solicitous of past friends."

"As I recall, our last encounter was less than friendly."

"Those of our blood are fewer than a handful, Gilda. We must learn to make peace with each other. We greeted the turning of this century in each other's company; I thought perhaps we might do the same for this millennium which is on everyone's lips."

Gilda watched his eyes as he'd spoken. They still glittered with the sullen anger he'd always harbored. Samuel's dark blond hair was masked almost completely by a narrow-brimmed hat which he wore at a rakish tilt. His wiry build rippled with tension beneath a raincoat with a short cape. The affectation made his shoulders appear much broader than Gilda knew them to be. She tried to push into his thoughts to discern the true reason he'd sought her out, but he carefully blocked her.

"For some reason, Samuel, you've always felt I cheated you. It's as if I were the favored child and you were somehow left out. I don't know why you've fixed this sentiment on me, nor do I care."

"You will care, Gilda my girl."

"I only care that you stop leaping into my life as if I owed you some form of retribution."

Samuel's bellowing laugh was riddled with strands of his hatred. Two men lingering in front of the metal-shuttered doorway of a bodega had glanced in their direction nervously, then ambled up the street to another spot. Gilda remembered the way he'd always clung to the idea that he was the victim, even when he was inflicting pain.

When they'd first met, Gilda was new to their life and still learning the mores and responsibilities of her power. But she knew immediately that Samuel was one who believed in nothing but his own gain, his own life. And wherever he'd fallen into error, he found someone else to blame. They were connected by blood that had turned sour, and Gilda was weary of trying to clean Samuel's wounds.

"The follies of your life are your own. Leave me out of them," Gilda said. The chill of her disaffection made her voice flat.

"Fine. If you insist. I'd always thought there was fairness about you, Gilda. I'm sure I'm not mistaken."

Samuel had turned on his heel and disappeared into the darkness, leaving Gilda to continue on her way home with a rising sense of ill-defined anxiety. Samuel had drawn her into battle twice in the past century. She had no doubt he intended to do the same again, sometime soon.

She veered off of Broadway down to West End Avenue, where grass sloped gently downward from the city street to the brackish river. The soft flowing of the water played in her ears, obscuring the city sound to her left and stirring her already bubbling uneasiness. She focused her attention to steel herself against the discomfort of the running water of the Hudson River so she could enjoy the textured darkness of the tree-lined avenue.

Ahead of her, hidden from the streetlight by the shadows of a thick maple tree, Gilda saw a man leaning against the park fence. Her body tensed, but she felt no fear. It wasn't Samuel. This was a mortal, in his twenties, strongly built and obviously up to no good. He wore a sweatsuit several sizes too large, but that did not conceal his muscled arms from her. The cap pulled down over his brow, meant to hide his features, only exposed his vulnerability to Gilda. Gilda slowed her steps momentarily, then thought: he's just a man.

A surprise flood of anger washed over her. She'd only recently understood such anger could be hers. Her mother, Fulani features hemmed into a placid gaze, had not been allowed that luxury. She'd been a slave, admonished to be grateful. As a child Gilda had not understood: the master, who owned all and was responsible for everyone, never showed anger; his wife, whom he pampered and worshipped oppressively, was angry all the time. As was the overseer who regularly vented his anger on black flesh. But blacks were not thought to have anger any more than a mule or a tree cut down for kindling.

Gilda looked quickly behind her and saw several apartment dwellers moving casually past their windows, and a couple approaching a little more than a block behind her. No sign of Samuel, but the young man stood ahead of her under the maple, his intentions leering out from behind an empty grin.

Gilda's step was firm. She wondered what drove men—black, white, rich, poor, alive or otherwise—to need to leap out at women from the darkness. As she walked past he spoke low, almost directly in her ear, "Hey, Mama, don't walk so fast."

Gilda continued on, hoping he would take his loss and shut up.

He didn't. "Aw, Mama, come on. Be nice to me."

The wheedling in his voice scraped and scratched at her. That sound had been the undercurrent of every conversation she'd had with Samuel over the past one hundred years. His demands for her help, his threats to harm her, his pleas for her sympathy were all delivered in the same falsely pitiful pitch. She'd side-stepped Samuel for years. They were, after all, connected by blood.

We're connected by blood too, Gilda thought, as she watched the young black man waiting. She understood that the poverty she saw around her ground people into hopelessness. She, herself, fought each day to resist the predatory impulse which seemed able to ease feelings of desperation. In the young man before her she recognized his surrender to that impulse. Like Samuel, he reeked of his rancid enjoyment of power over someone else he considered weaker, unworthy. An assault in the dark was the substitution for truly taking power.

Anger speared her, leaving a metallic taste in her mouth. Where were the words for what she felt?

Gilda stopped and turned to him, smiling as she remembered the words of an irate Chicago waitress she'd overheard decades before: "I am not your mama. If I were, I would have drowned you at birth."

She walked on. He caught up. "Why you bitches so hard. Come on, sistah, give me a break!"

Gilda continued walking. She had no desire to end the night with angry blood.

"Come on, sistah, let me see that smile again." With that, he seized her arm. His grip would have bruised another, but Gilda shook free easily, leaving him off balance. In a smooth reach he snatched at her close-cropped hair, hoping to pull her into the darkness.

The image of Effie, waiting in their rooms, her sinewy form concealed in shadow, flashed through Gilda's mind. A low moan sounded in the back of her throat. She could almost feel her slim fingers clenched around his neck, snapping the connection to the spine. She replaced that sensation with the memory of a hot night thirty years before—Florida in 1950. She'd been sitting in an after-hours club watching the fighter show how he'd whipped a Tampa boy who said boxing was just a "coon show."

Gilda smiled again as she raised her left fist in perfect form and smashed it into the man's jaw. He fell unconscious to the cracked pavement, half-sprawled on the thin city grass.

Gilda lifted him from the street and held him to her as the couple she had seen earlier passed by. Once they were several paces away she lowered the man to the ground so he sat against the maple tree. She knelt low, hiding him from the street, and smoothly sliced the flesh behind his ear with her fingernail. His eyes opened in shock, and Gilda held him in the grip of her hands and her mind. He was pinned against the tree, its rough bark biting into his shirt as Gilda rummaged amongst his thoughts. Confusion replaced shock, then rage followed. Unable to move, the young man bellowed internally. His ideas were petty, self-centered, ignorant of any world except the small circle in which he traveled. The history Gilda knew, the triumphs she'd seen all meant nothing to him. Gilda had not felt so unrelated to a mortal since she'd taken on this life. In his eyes she observed the same deadness she often saw in Samuel's: they looked inward, were always scavenging. They never really saw.

Gilda pressed her lips to the cut. Blood had begun to seep out onto his sweatshirt. The flesh was soft and smelled of sweet soap. Gilda could imagine the boy he'd been, when he was still able to imagine himself a part of the larger world. She drew her share of the blood from him swiftly, barely enjoying the warmth as it washed over her. His anger began to swell inside of her, wiping away the sensation of his youth. She was engorged yet continued taking the blood, feeling no need to stop, no need to leave something for him.

At the final moment she pulled back, lifted her lips from his neck, and looked into his almost dead eyes. She touched his nearly empty mind, searching for a tiny place where there was no anger or hatred. There she planted the understanding of what it could mean to really feel love toward a sister, and from that love a connection to the rest of the world. In the shallow cavern of his thoughts she left him one sensation to live for, one goal to strive for as she held her hand to seal the wound. His pulse was faint but soon became steady. She lifted him gently and rested him on the park bench, placing his arms casually behind his head, as if he were only napping. She drew the cap back so it rested on the crown of his head but left his dark face open and smooth in the dim light. His lips were no longer curled in a smirk. She could see the young man he'd been, the young man he might still be.

As she rose to leave, Gilda was glad she had such a good memory. "Yeah, Joe Louis was a heck of a fighter," she said aloud.

She knew it would not be so simple with Samuel. A century of bitterness and jealousy, left over from times even Gilda couldn't remember, festered, fueling itself. She looked down at the young man and hoped his bitterness would end here.

Gilda continued downtown, her sense of dread building. Samuel's words were like a prickly burr against her skin. Turning them over, back and forth, she searched for reasons Samuel would return at this particular time. The young man she'd left on the bench had probably lived all of his life under the sour message implying his worthlessness. He made victims of others out of ignorance. Not just ignorance. Vanity! Gilda thought. She probed the air around her looking for Samuel's thoughts, trying to discern his presence. She perceived only apartment dwellers and the homeless who slept in the park. It was a kind of vanity that drove Samuel and the young man. They could not be one of many, but only one—always alone, always outlawed. And that fooled them into thinking they were on top.

Her recollection of the last time Samuel had burst into her life did not comfort Gilda. For a moment it had seemed as if he'd forgotten their past, had learned to appreciate his special place in the world. He'd appeared in much the same way as he'd done this evening, with no warning, on a public street. Then he'd been more devious, trying to lull Gilda into a sense of goodwill. Her wariness had lingered and was proven justified. The battle between them had gone on for several hours, leaving both with gruesome injuries. Gilda had not wanted to fight him, or to kill him. It had been a draw, and Samuel had retreated when he understood that Gilda could not be easily destroyed. Gilda shuddered. There can be no fairness in a fight between us, she thought.

Fair. The word resonated in Gilda's mind. Something about the way he'd said the word several times. She felt the skin of her entire body become an antenna tingling with input. And then she understood. Samuel had said she was not fair—not light-skinned. Then he'd said there was "fairness about you." He was talking about Effie. In some cultures, the name Effie meant fair. Effie herself had told Gilda that when they first met. Samuel had come to hurt Gilda, just as she suspected, but he'd do that by hurting Effie.

The chill that had settled on Gilda curled under at the edges of the flame that shot through her body. She now knew why the image of Effie had shown her in shadow. Anger pulsed through Gilda, leaving no room for caution. She knew Effie had powers at least as strong as her own, yet fear for Effie's safety seared her heart. She pushed a warning through the air toward their home as she turned swiftly southward, then disappeared inside the wind blowing off the river.

TO BE CONTINUED...

APOSTATE PRINCESS RETURNS TO PLOVIDIV

JUDITH KATZ

Rumor in the streets and back alleys of the Kazimierz district had it that Princess Eugenia Vanstazia fled Poland for her native Bulgaria because she had become, of all things, a Jew. I believed that she was no longer a practicing Christian; in fact, I knew better than any that she was not. And it was logical that if someone such as the princess became a Jew, she would, of course, leave Poland. Who, with the wherewithal to do so, would not?

But in these trying times, a Bulgarian Jewess wasn't much better off than a Polish one. Russian soldiers lost their minds as quickly on the streets of Plovidiv as they did in Cracow when they caught scent of Jewish blood, and there was no telling what they would do if one of their royal ladies had made a sudden shift in orthodoxies. Here in Cracow the princess enjoyed a certain celebrity, but also a kind of curiosity-soaked privacy; in Plovidiv she was simply celebrated and enjoyed no privacy at all.

No, if Princess Eugenia had it in mind to be a freer Jew, the place for her to escape to would be England or the United States. As far as I could tell, she wasn't fleeing from religious persecution at all. The Princess Eugenia was, I am certain, fleeing from me.

Though I was not highborn like Princess Eugenia, here in Cracow, especially in my current situation, I often felt like misplaced royalty. My father was one of the few Jews in Poland who was allowed to keep his timberlands until his death, some years before the Russian revolution. When he died, my father passed his land on to my brother Stephan. Seeing the sanguine-colored writing on the wall, my brother, who had an affinity for city life, fancy clothes, and fine-born Christian ladies, sold the land. He received an excellent price for it, and although he could have gotten away with giving me much less, he was a kind-hearted, generous man and divided the profits exactly in two. He presented me with a dozen heavy cloth sacks stuffed to the brim with gold and silver.

"If you are wise, you'll invest this," he told me. "If you must stay here, start a business. When you can bear these muddy streets no longer, join me in New York."

I thought about New York, but to tell you the truth, muddy Cracow had been my home for so long, I couldn't imagine leaving it. And so I took my share of the timberland profits and bought a two-story building on Jozefa Street. I made the upstairs into a comfortable home, with good wood furniture, a piano, and lovely Persian rugs. I put paintings on the walls and, when they were in season, kept flowers in every room. Downstairs I opened a plush little teahouse, warm and dark, where ladies could come for an afternoon of social chatter and men could come with secret ladies and have the privacy of a club. I filled the shop with exotic green plants, and tucked tiny tables into dark corners where romantic dealings could be done.

I hired two girls, one to wait table by day, the other by night. I prepared the pastries myself, and on winter days, which in Cracow were long and damp and not very pleasant, I made soups and stews. These, served with fresh bread from Zimkeh the Baker, made life very pleasant for my Kazimierz customers.

Back then I was quite attractive, round and rosy-cheeked, always ready to laugh at a good joke. There were also rumors about my hidden wealth, and more than one matchmaker knocked on my door. But no one except my brother knew exactly how much money I had. Besides, by the time Princess Eugenia burst into my little shop, I knew very well that I would never marry. For like my brother, I had a taste for fine-born Christian ladies; they were often married themselves and always discreet, and they never asked more from me than a private evening in my little flat. This was usually followed by a jeweled brooch or pair of earrings left for me on the night table and a brief note trusting that I would exercise the utmost discretion. Once or twice these trysts were followed by small bouquets of roses, but except in passing, I never saw any of these lovers again.

I found this suited me perfectly, and I was certain I wouldn't become any man's wife.

I was not a devout Jew, but I knew what side my bread was buttered on. I knew it was best for business if I made an appearance from time to time in *shul,* to reassure my customers that I was truly one of them. I willingly spent an occasional Shabbes evening up in the women's balcony, tucked behind those velvet curtains, listening to the muffled sound of the rabbi as he spoke for me to God. I hated the barrier between me and the men, but in spite of it, I enjoyed the uplifting feeling an evening of prayer can bring, even when a person is walled off from the real action. Later, I used the privacy of that stuffy women's balcony in Szeroka Street's grand synagogue to enjoy the pleasure of Princess Eugenia's company. But I shall share this enchantment with you in good time.

At first I thought she was coming to sell me her tiara or her fancy fur coat. Often, exiled royalty came to me in the mistaken assumption that because I am Jewish I must be a usurer; they offered up their valuables for a short-term loan. I knew for certain that she was after more than a cup of tea and one of my splendid nut pastries. She was taller than any other customer in the shop and seemed dressed more for a night at the opera than for an afternoon of chatting and sipping. She wore dark glasses and black gloves that seemed to cover many large rings on both her hands. Her hair was wrapped in a sleek satin turban. A diamond the size of a teardrop hung from each of her ears. She had a black fur coat pulled around her like a bathrobe, and for the briefest moment I found myself wondering if she was wearing any clothing underneath. In a minute my mind was put at ease, for the princess flung off her coat, placed it on the back of a chair, and sat in what looked for all intents and purposes like a tight-fitting black evening gown. On any other woman, the effect would have been gaudy and cheap. Princess Eugenia Vanstazia looked only elegant, there at a marble-topped table in the far corner of my shop on Jozefa Street in the heart of Jewish Cracow at two o'clock on a Monday afternoon.

The young girl who worked during the day started straight for the princess. I held her back, as I straightened my apron and loosened my hair.

"I'll take care of this one myself," I said. I made my way to her table and cleared my throat. "What will the princess have this afternoon?"

She looked at me panic-stricken. "Have we met?"

"Princess Vanstazia, we have not yet had the pleasure, but I don't believe that there is one person in the city of Cracow who would not know you instantly the moment she saw you."

She removed her dark glasses and carefully studied my face. "You are the proprietor. You are Anna Davidovich."

I nodded.

"You are the very person I was hoping to see. Have the girl get us each a cup of tea and then do sit down."

As the other customers in the shop were well taken care of, I signaled to the young woman and had her bring us not only tea but a tray of sweets as well. Then I pulled a chair up close to my guest. "The princess should know right away that I am not in the business of lending money or buying jewelry."

She looked at me as if I'd spoken to her in Chinese. "I beg your pardon? I have plenty of cash at the moment, and even if my pockets were completely empty," she said, pulling a glove off her left hand and wiggling her fingers in front of me, "I would never part with any one of these. For each was given me by a lover." The rings shimmered in the dim light of my shop "Sadly," she continued, "of each of them, it is all I have left."

I thought for a moment to tell her that I had a similar collection of romantic trinkets at home, but thought better of it. The girl appeared with a silver teapot and set it on our table. A minute later she returned with two delicate china cups, cream, lemon, and a platter of my delectable cookies. I placed one myself on the princess' plate.

She appeared horrified. "My dear, I never take sweets —"

I put my hand on her wrist. "This you must, dear princess, for I have made them myself only this morning. And I promise, you will never taste another like it here or in Plovidiv."

"I'm sure," said the princess as she took a tiny bite, "but let me tell you the reason I've come."

Now I wondered if the other familiar exchange would take place. I considered very carefully as I studied her whether one evening of pleasure with the glamorous princess might possibly be enough. Which of her amorous trinkets might she pass on to me? Which would I desire? She blew into her tea quite carefully and then looked up at me with worried eyes. She touched my hand discreetly and leaned in toward my ear.

"You must teach me to read and speak the Hebrew prayers," she whispered.

I sat up, completely startled. "I?"

"But who else?" Her eyes flashed. "Each rabbi in this tiny town has looked at me as if I present them a practical joke."

I poured more tea into her china cup. "What about the woman

north of here who has made herself a rabbi?"

The princess sipped her tea and took another nibble from a cookie. She dabbed her lips with an immaculate white linen hanky. "If indeed she exists, she is over one hundred years old by now, and that century-old hag lives in a *shtetl* so tiny no one like me could ever find her. No, there's no question. You are to be my teacher."

I looked the princess up and down. I didn't know who sent her to me, but whoever it was was not wrong. After my mother died, it was I who blessed the candles every Friday night. Since my brother had taken no interest in anything holy, it was left to me to learn the letters and prayers, for my father needed someone to pray Kaddish for him when he was no longer alive. I had, in fact, said the Kaddish for the required weeks after he passed away, and from time to time, as I have said, subsequently went and sat in the women's balcony on Szeroka Street. The leap from Yiddish, which I read and spoke fluently, wasn't such a great one to Hebrew—although truth be told, they are completely different languages—and so it was true that in the matter of the simple prayers, I could be somewhat expert and provide the princess with the help she needed. But I wasn't ready to provide my services yet. "Since when, Princess Vanstazia, do the Russian Orthodox pray in Hebrew?"

She tapped a gloved finger against the table. "You verge on impertinent, Miss Davidovich. The Russian Orthodox do not pray in Hebrew. Jews such as yourself pray in Hebrew. I want to learn to say the Hebrew prayers because before the next month is out, I must know what it is to be a Jew."

I could only stare at the princess with my mouth agape. "You're joking!"

"Now you sound like those tiresome rabbis. I have never in my life been more serious—"

"A woman of your stature, choosing to become a Jew? Why on earth?"

The princess took a long draw of her tea and licked her lips.

She reached into her beaded purse and brought out a card with the name and address of one of the fanciest hotels in the old city. "Come to me in my rooms this evening after eleven o'clock and I will tell you everything."

"I don't close the shop until midnight, Princess Vanstazia."

"Then I will expect you at half-past midnight," she told me. She wrapped her fur coat around her, and without leaving so much as a *groszy* on the table, she was out the door.

As you might imagine, I was very distracted for the hours remaining between the princess' dramatic exit and the time at which we were to meet. The shop became busy, and I was occupied with many customers. Yet I could not stop wondering why anyone, but most particularly a Bulgarian princess who could do anything that her great wealth would allow, would want to be a Jew. To do so in Poland at this juncture in time seemed unnecessarily dangerous and old-fashioned to me. For one thing, there was, as I have stated, the place of Jews in Poland at this moment in the universe, which is to say nowhere if not under the threat of some peasant's pitchfork or some Cossack's bloody saber. Let us not forget my brother and his decision to turn timber into gold and fly to a warmer, sweeter climate where a Jew might be spat upon, but the possibility of his becoming minced meat was slightly less likely.

There was also, as I have told you, the unfortunate condition of women in our strictest religious configurations: in life, to sit behind a suffocating curtain; in death, to hold up our husband's feet in heaven. True, with the enlightenment upon us, with Jewish men shaving beards and shedding frock coats for snappy suit jackets and starched collars, and women tossing aside sheitels and kerchiefs in favor of our own curly locks, one could see that a Jewish woman might imagine herself to be free. But that Jewish woman could hardly be said to feel free in the synagogue. Her very freedom depended upon her ability to close the door on much of her spiritual past.

I went over each possibility and question with mathematical precision, until it was time to close the shop and meet the princess in her rooms. By then I could come to only one conclusion: somewhere in Cracow the princess kept a Jewish lover. For reasons I could not fathom she wanted to marry him, and in order to marry him, she must convert. But even this, the most logical conclusion, made no sense. Why would someone with her wealth and power change for him? In this day and age specifically, why would anyone bother? Unless, of course, the man was a great learned teacher, a rabbi, but then why wouldn't he teach the princess himself?

Such were my thoughts as I closed up shop and retired upstairs to change into clothes more befitting a Hebrew tutor than a teashop owner. I left a light on in my apartment, stepped into a taxi, and was taken straightaway up past the castle to the old city and the steps of the Europeski Hotel.

The desk clerk rang up to Princess Eugenia's room and then signaled me toward the elevator. "Room thirty-four," he said in a discreet voice. "The princess suggests that you knock once."

The man who ran the elevator directed me to the left, and I knocked as I was told on the door of number thirty-four. I expected a butler to answer and was so surprised when the princess herself let me in. She was wearing another tight-fitting black dress with a green silk robe over it. On her feet she wore black satin slippers. The rings on both her hands were in full view.

"Miss Davidovich, you have arrived!" She swept me into the foyer and took my coat herself. "Are you hungry, Miss Davidovich? I've had them send up an array of things you might like to eat." She thrust me further into her suite. In the center room there were two plush velvet-covered couches, a rocking chair, and a fireplace in which burned a sweet, small fire. On a sideboard by one of the couches was a splendid midnight supper: fruits cut and peeled, caviar, smoked fishes, breads, and in the center, an open bottle of champagne.

"Princess Vanstazia—"

"Eugenia—"

"Princess Eugenia, I thought I was here to offer you my small knowledge of the Hebrew language."

"In my country, Miss Davidovich, we find that scholarly pursuits are best met with a full stomach."

I sat on the couch and watched as the princess poured me a glass of champagne.

"I thought you must come with a cadre of servants, Princess Eugenia."

She threw her head back and laughed. "That is presupposing a person has the servants in the first place. I may be royalty," she said, handing me the goblet, the tiny bubbles dancing about like magic, "and even have the capital to live like this, but I'm afraid that means spreading my own caviar and pouring my own wine."

I sipped and watched as she spread a slice of brown bread with the thick black fish eggs. She offered it to me. I shook my head.

"Before we begin our lesson, Princess Eugenia, if you will permit me, I have been worrying myself all evening trying to determine why you want to learn the Hebrew prayers. I assumed it was because you had a lover and this lover wanted you to marry but in order to marry you must become a Jew—"

"Marry? I?" The princess looked stricken. "To a man?"

I nodded.

The princess burst out laughing. "You believed that I would become Jewish in order to marry a man?"

Oh, and then she laughed again, and when she did this time it was all I could do to keep from taking her into both my arms and kissing her right there in the middle of her sitting room. She brought her face very close to my own. "It isn't marriage that wants me to claim the Jewish faith, my friend." She took a bite of her caviar and sat down on the couch beside me. "No no, it isn't marriage at all."

"What is it then?" The drink's sharp bubbles cut into my throat.

"Not marriage, dear Anna Davidovich, but mortality."

"Mortality?"

"Yes, my friend. Fear and knowledge of my own death."

"Are you ill?"

"I've never been healthier. But tempus fugit, Anna Davidovich. Time flies, and I become old in the blink of an eye."

I looked at the princess dumbfounded.

"How old do you think I am?"

"You can't be a day past thirty—"

"In six weeks I shall be exactly thirty, and that is my point. In six weeks my life will be half over—what do I have to show for it?"

I was perplexed to say the least. "For one thing, you have a small principality in Bulgaria. You, theoretically, have wealth beyond what I can imagine, and a vast array of knowledge in many subjects, academic and otherwise."

"All that may be true, my friend Anna Davidovich, but there is one thing I lack. My life is half over, and I have no spiritual recourse for the end of my days."

Now I was completely baffled. "Why not go back to your Russian roots?"

Her eyes flashed. "What is that but old men with beards and jeweled hats swinging incense in all directions."

"What is Judaism but more men with beards?"

She looked at me aghast. "My dear Anna Davidovich! Men with beards, yes, but also the scrolled Torah containing the five books of Moses, the Holy Ark, rabbis who spin and dance—"

"Those same spinning rabbis, I am sorry to tell you Princess Eugenia, would sooner spin off a cliff as look at you—"

"Oh, I'm entirely aware of that, my friend. The point is, Jew or not a Jew, I wish to learn the Hebrew prayers in order to make a spiritual life of my own—the letters are the key to the door of transcendence. I can tell by looking at them. Now I must know their secrets."

I sipped my champagne and studied this princess in candlelight. Was it her madness that made her so beautiful to me?

"To understand me, you must know something of my past,

Miss Davidovich. I come from a long line of religious dabblers. I have studied the religion of theosophy at the knee of Madame Blavatsky herself for a year. The concept is intriguing, and I'm not entirely convinced it isn't a useful spiritual practice for some— but sadly, not for me. My mother, Princess Iphegenia, consulted Greek oracles for years. She keeps an altar to the goddess Isis in her private chambers of her Sofia apartment to this day. My brother, Prince Pitor, frequently seeks the counsel of astrologers, and you may have heard the strange news that our father, Prince Gregor, was one of the few people in the entire Russian empire who actually encouraged Tsar Nicholas to keep that mad monk Rasputin close at hand. We have in our family done everything but sacrifice live animals in the palace courtyard." She burst out with that laugh again. "So it should come as no surprise to any-one that I want the key to your religion. Perhaps, you see, I shall learn to make it mine."

I heard her say these words, I even understood them, but all I wanted to do by the time she was done was throw my champagne glass over my shoulder and kiss her on her crazed mouth. "When shall we begin?" I asked, my voice barely a whisper.

She sat beside me on the couch and took out a small book of Hebrew prayers. "Right now," she told me. "Isn't there a prayer one says to welcome in the night?"

Princess Eugenia proved an excellent student, even as I felt less and less secure as her teacher. Each night I went to call on her. She provided me with delicious sustenance, and I in turn taught her what I could about the Hebrew alphabet, the various blessings, even the stories I knew from the Torah. She often touched my shoulders and legs, leaned in close to me over the prayer book, but never did she make as if to kiss me. I, thinking it would take more nerve to kiss a princess than I possessed, decided to enjoy the electricity between us that intellectual stimulation can bring, but left the impassioned embraces for another world.

Then, on the third Thursday evening I arrived at her rooms, the princess greeted me with distraction and led me into her sitting room. There was only strong coffee and a loaf of black bread on the table, which surprised me. "We've no time to lose," she said. "Sit here beside me and put me through my paces. Tomorrow evening you must take me to the synagogue to pray."

I poured myself a cup of coffee and sat beside the princess. "Is there a special occasion?" I asked.

She seemed annoyed. "Why, it is your Jewish Sabbath. Isn't that occasion enough?"

I sipped my coffee and stared at her. If only she would forget this religious fervor and beg me to kiss her. "If the princess will permit, it has been my Sabbath for some Friday nights before this one. Why are you so urgent to go to synagogue now?"

She snapped her prayer book shut and stood up. She towered over me in that moment. "Miss Davidovich, you verge on the impertinent. I have not requested to go to synagogue before tomorrow because I have not felt ready before now. Open to page forty-five. I begin by reciting the prayer to bring in the Sabbath queen."

"Very well," I said, and sat back to listen. Princess Eugenia of Plovidiv recited her Hebrew as if she were born speaking it. Such was the case with all of the prayers, and while I was dazzled, the princess seemed merely pleased and self-assured.

"I'll meet you outside your shop at 5:30," she told me. "We will walk together from there."

"The synagogue is just around my corner," I said. "You can come a bit later if you like."

"I'll come at 5:30 and not one minute after," she told me. "When a lady of my stature enters a place of worship she must be absolutely on time and absolutely discreet."

For all my experiences with women, never before had I accompanied a love interest to pray. Needless to say, I was beside myself with nervousness and anticipated pleasure. Imagine it, a princess who might some day kiss me, even my hand, would sit beside me in those hateful wooden pews and together we would read our Hebrew and pray for some salvation. I could hardly contain myself.

As she said she would, she arrived at my shop at 5:30 exactly. The day girl was just closing up for Shabbat. I wore my best black dress, which was quite simple compared with the princess', though to be honest, her clothing was more subdued than any I had seen her in before. She wore a broad-brimmed black hat and a thick veil, and a black tasteful fur coat. She held out her elbow to me. Together we walked into the Szeroka Street *shul* and up the stairs to our confinement.

Heads turned but then turned back. The service began. I must tell you now that never before was my religious experience so religious as when I sat beside the Princess Eugenia. I do not know how long we sat, or what the rabbi may have said in our behalf. I can only tell you that it thrilled me to sit beside the princess as she confidently said her blessings, but when she took my hand and held it underneath her book of prayer, ah, no event with God in its center ever pleased me more. This is not to say that the princess did not complain. "It's stuffy up here. One can barely hear the rabbi," she whispered.

"That is why I don't come here often," I whispered back.

"But if one is to have a spirit home after one is dead..."

I shook my head. "After one of us is dead, that is to say, one of us *women,* according to that man in front of this curtain and other men like him, we are to become footstools to our husbands in heaven."

"So you have said." The princess sighed sadly, then she leaned very close to me and squeezed my hand. "Let us pray," she whispered, and I whispered back, "Indeed."

After services, the princess stole down the stairs with me and out the door. "I must say, it was a disappointment in some respects," she confided.

"How is that?"

"I expected to feel a bit more uplifted than I do just now."

"Princess Eugenia, come back to my rooms. I'll feed you a supper and we can talk all about this."

"If you insist," the princess sighed.

"I do," I said, "I do."

Once in my apartment I prepared a table fit for any princess— cold chicken, sweet *challa,* pickles, and sweet Jewish wine. The princess sat and ate with great relish. I leaned back in my chair, eager to hear her complaints about our time in the synagogue. But this was not what the princess had in mind. She took a handful of bread and leaned across the table to me. "It is, I understand, considered a great good deed to make love on the Sabbath."

I somehow managed to swallow a sip of wine. "Why yes, for a man and woman to do so is considered a great good deed."

"Do you think it is only for a man and woman?"

I put my glass down and looked carefully into the princess' eyes. "I think the general idea is that the husband pleases the wife on the Sabbath and may also propagate the race."

The princess took a sip of her wine. "Might the student not at this time also choose to please the teacher?"

I sat back in my chair and pushed the hair from in front of my face. "If the student wished to do so, the teacher could hardly object."

"Come here then, Miss Davidovich." The princess held her arms open to me and I walked into them. *"Shabbat shalom,"* she said, and kissed my mouth.

"Shabbat shalom, Princess Eugenia." I kissed her in return. "You have learned very well."

In the morning, as I expected, the princess was gone, but there was no note or trinket. There was, however, her small prayer book, which I could not believe she left as a love token. I prepared my morning tea and a small breakfast but I could barely eat. At sundown I hailed a *droshky* and went to the princess' hotel. As I made my way to the elevator the desk clerk stopped me.

"I'm afraid the princess is no longer a guest at our hotel." He shook his head sadly.

"Where is she?" I was panicked, but I kept my breath.

"I've no idea, Miss Davidovich. At about eleven o'clock this morning, her brother, Prince Pitor, came to pick her up in a motor car. It caused quite a stir up here as you might imagine. Two servants took all of her belongings, the prince paid the bill, and they were off."

"But where did she go?"

"I've no idea, Miss Davidovich, as I have said."

I looked down at the small prayer book. "This belongs to the princess."

"Well, keep it, why don't you, until you meet again. You're just as likely as I am to see her, wouldn't you agree?"

I flipped through the pages, hailed another *droshky*, and headed home.

I spent many days searching my soul for clues and messages from the Princess Eugenia. I took to going to *shul* in the vain hope that I would find her there sitting amongst the common Jewish women, but soon I gave this practice up, for I was tempted then to pray to God for her return. I kept her prayer book by my bed for a time, and finally stowed it away with the baubles and trinkets I'd received from past lovers. Still, in the mornings I woke thinking about her, and at night hers was the last name I called before I drifted off to sleep. Weeks passed in this way, and then months, and still my heart felt smashed to bits. I took no pleasure in other women, though many sought me out. I spent my waking hours working and walking. How often, as I trod the muddy path along the Vistula, did I think I caught a glimpse of my princess, a shimmer of black silk in the far distance, followed by that wicked laugh. I wrote to my brother Stephan in New York. He wired me back: SELL THE SHOP AND COME HERE, ALL WILL BE WELL. WITH LOVE, S.

I thought this over carefully. True, Poland was my home, but it had become a lonely hovel. The rain and mud had lost their charm. New faces might help me, a new language and a new land. My brother had a home on a huge park in the middle of the city. My life could be better there, though no less sad.

I found a buyer for my business, and in the bargain I threw in my wonderful furnishings and paintings. I wired my brother, purchased a steamer ticket, and packed: one trunk full of clothing, the other full of books and photographs. The last I packed was a carpetbag, in which I placed my most precious belongings. I wondered if I shouldn't sell the jewelry my lovers had left me but thought better of it. If prospects didn't change for me, at least I would have a glittery set of amorous tokens to look back upon. Finally, I considered the princess' prayer book. I turned it over and over in my hands, then placed it into the carpetbag as well. She had broken my heart, but with this trip I would forget her. Oh, I was certain of that.

The next day I dressed for my journey in a fine gray skirt and matching jacket, high leather shoes, gloves, and a smart straw hat. The *droshky* driver loaded my luggage, and I hopped in behind him. We were off to the train station. I would embark from there to Gdansk and then sail to America. At the very moment the driver was about to snap his whip and set his pony trotting, a young man in a blue uniform came peddling full speed on his bicycle, right at us.

"Miss Davidovich, stop! Wait! I've a wire for you! I've a wire for you all the way from Bulgaria!"

The *droshky* driver halted his pony, and I took the envelope from the messenger's gloved hand. I reached into my bag and found him ten *groszy*. He tipped his hat, hopped back upon his bicycle, and rode away. I held tight to the wire. "What are you waiting for?" I asked the *droshky* driver. "The train leaves in thirty minutes. We must hurry."

"Yes, Miss," he said, and snapped his whip loudly in the air.

I waited until I was settled in my compartment and the train was moving until I dared read the Bulgarian princess' wire. I took a last look at Cracow as it rolled by my window. When we crossed the river, I slipped the telegram out of my bag, slipped a finger under the seal, and broke it open. MY DEAR ANNA DAVIDOVICH, it started, SHALOM, SHALOM.

TO BE CONTINUED...

FEAR

RANDYE LORDON

Frieda says the only way to rid yourself of fear is to confront it directly. Frieda is, without a doubt, one of the most together women I have ever known, so when we were out one night, a group of us, and she said that, and suggested that one of the gals make herself a list of the things that scared her, well you know, I went straight home and made my own list. I put down everything that scares me. *Everything.*

I must have had close to 150 things on that list. I wrote down everything from cellulite to crime, and under crime I listed *another* fifty things I was afraid of, for example being the victim of a car-jacking, or coming in and finding burglars in my house like Mrs. Thornton did when I was a little girl and they tied her up and tried to set her on fire. Fortunately, she kept blowing out the match and her son came home before they did more than singe her wig and eyebrows, but she was never the same after that, and I certainly understand why. Crime can make you crazy, you know.

And acts of God. At least that's what I think they would call it, or maybe it was mechanical failure—you remember that plane in Hawaii? The top sheared off in the front like it was a convertible, and something like four people were sucked out of their seats and pulled into the engine? I've heard that the woman in the seat right behind the row that was blown away will never be okay, just like Mrs. Thornton, and I don't blame her. Flying is hard enough, without the damned thing becoming a pop-top.

I used to have a job that required I travel a lot. Finally, after five years of it, I had to leave. I couldn't do it anymore. I mean, seriously, it got to the point where I could not fly.

Anyway, I made up my list and showed it to Frieda (like she really wanted an intimate look inside my fears). Actually, when I first started writing the list and told the people at work what I was doing, one of my co-workers revealed to a whole roomful of people that he was afraid of marshmallows. He couldn't explain why he was afraid of them, only that he was. Poor fool had at least sixteen bags of marshmallows stuffed in his desk drawers by the end of the day. How could you be afraid of marshmallows? And who would admit it to a group of people, especially people you work with?

Then again, by telling the roomful of people and having them respond the way they did, he got over his fear, which is exactly what Frieda said. *Things are always bigger in your head.* That's another one of her maxims. When I showed Frieda my list, she read through it real carefully, not saying a word, but nodding every now and then.

After what seemed like forever, she handed me back the list and asked how I was doing confronting the problems. She didn't tell me that half of my list was absurd, like my mother and sister did when I showed it to them, and she didn't tell me I was a moron for being afraid of cellulite, like my best friend Debra Ann said. Understand, it's not like I'm afraid of cellulite like it's a disease or anything, but I had this aunt when I was a kid who had the worst cellulite you could possibly imagine. I mean, we used to call her Aunt Tushy-bubbles. At the pool, when we were real little, she used to make me touch the craters and she'd say, "See stupid, flesh, that's all, flesh. You wait. One of these days..." Oh my God, if you saw the women in my family, you'd understand that I am one breath away from those tushy-bubbles, one breath away from becoming my aunt, or my mother, or my *grand-mother*. Which is a whole *other* thing I don't even want to talk about.

But Frieda was great. We talked about the global thing of trying to confront my fears instead of focusing on each and every detail. For example, like my fear of laps. It's not exactly a fear, per se, but I avoid them like the plague. Not my own, other people's. I mean, I couldn't avoid my own lap, could I? Unless I never sat, which would be impossible. But I hate laps. It must go back to when I was a little girl and our parents had Alvin baby-sit. My Lord, he was gross. He used to bounce us on his knee and, well I'm sure you can use your imagination, thank you very much. He even did it in front of our parents, bounce-bounce-bounce, like he was a horsey and we were the *wee equestrians*. That's what he used to call us. In the meantime, he'd be rubbing his thingie against our fannies. But that doesn't matter, what matters is I don't *like* laps. It's not that I'm afraid of them so much, which is what Frieda and I discovered when we were talking that time, so I was able to scratch laps right off my list. It was very freeing. I thought for the first time in my life, I thought, Hell, I can do anything I set my mind to.

I started dealing with the other things on my list, like small spaces, especially closets, fire—fire scares me a lot—projectile vomiting, frostbite, ferris wheels, restaurants, bugs—all bugs except, oddly enough, cockroaches. Flying. Ghosts. Stephen King stories. Cats. Loud noises. Public telephones. The Middle East. Public bathrooms. Rats. Salmonella. Tunnels. Explosions. Subways. Cancer. Joyce Carol Oates, Lord—the woman makes me cringe. Death. Worms. Parties. Public transportation in general. People. Constipation. Suffocation. Dentists. Lightning. Pierced body parts.

I have tried to conquer almost all of the fears on my list, at least those I could. See, something like frostbite I basically had addressed and didn't know it, as I never go out in the cold without extraordinary protection. Frieda and I went to a local animal shelter and with the help of one of their volunteers I actually played with the cats. I wear gloves whenever I touch public phones, but I can do it now. Public bathrooms? I tried one in a restaurant which is where I am sure I contracted eczema, but at least I tried it. I have never projectile vomited, or vomited at all, at least not since I was a kid, but I really think that if I were to find myself in a situation where I thought I might projectile vomit, I could do it and survive. See, all this is about surviving, you know what I mean?

More than anything else, I have learned I can do anything I put my mind to. I can tackle any problem. Anything. So, when I was offered a job with Willson, Newman, Loehman and McCoy, I knew I had to deal with my fear of flying. The job requires a lot of time out in the field, which means flying. A lot of flying.

The three weeks before I started the job were a nightmare. I couldn't sleep. Whenever I put my head down, my chest felt as if it was about to implode. I'd get the sweats and then the chills. Finally, I took drugs to fall asleep; my mind couldn't take it anymore. Only when I took the pills was I able to get more than twenty minutes at a stretch, but it was horrible because the whole time I had nightmares. Nightmares about me and the job and my family and people laughing at me. That's another thing I just hate. I hate it when people laugh at me. It's not a fear, just, you know, something that makes me really, really mad.

Penny Feitzer laughed at me in school once when we were in gym class. She thought the way I ran was funny and she got all the other kids to laugh at me and mock the way I ran. Now, come on, I just run like everyone else, but she had to make a thing out of it, call attention to me. *Bad* attention, not good attention. I just stopped running. I didn't care if the teacher failed me. Who cared about gym anyway? Besides, I got even with that little bitch.

My big brother was smoking a lot of grass then, and I took one of his joints and put it in her purse. I called her mother and told her that her daughter was dealing drugs. They didn't know me from Adam, so I didn't have to disguise my voice, but I could hear her mother seething on the other end of the line. Then they found the joint, and Penny got whipped by her father and grounded for a month. Senior year she wasn't even at school. They sent her away to boarding school for her last year, which was too bad, I guess, because it turned out that she was depressed; her folks didn't trust her and she had a hard time making friends at her new school, which I guess was real snotty. I heard she killed herself by slitting her wrists. I felt bad for her family when I heard that, but I guess she really brought it upon herself. She shouldn't have made me mad.

Penny was actually in a few of the nightmares I had when I was taking those pills to sleep. As a matter of fact, I was dreaming about her when I realized what I had to do if I was going to take this job at WNL&M.

See, my fear of flying isn't just that I'm afraid to fly. Oh no, I don't think it's just that for *anyone* who's afraid of flying. It's much more complex. I mean, what is the fear of flying? It's the fear of dying. The fear of falling out of the sky at speeds you can't even imagine. It's the fear that some religious zealot might decide to blow up a plane full of innocent people to prove a point no one cares about. It's the fear of exploding. The fear of not exploding, but seeing everyone around you explode and then having those ten or twenty seconds of panic as you're catapulted through the atmosphere to certain death. It's the fear of having your breath completely sucked out of you like you're nothing but a plastic bag. It's a fear of living through the crash and being engulfed in flames or toxic fumes. It's the fear of the hideous screams of hundreds of strangers bound to you forever in death. The fear of flying is the fear of seeing someone you love decapitated in the next seat while you remain unscathed.

Everyone's afraid of flying. They have to be, because it's the fear of death, and we're all afraid of death, aren't we?

So this dream I had was more like an epiphany. It showed me the way. I got up in the middle of the night and went immediately to my list because the dream led me to believe that I could, quite easily, find a way to confront all of my fears at the same time. The fear of flying, the fear of death, the fear of people, explosions, ghosts, fire, I mean all of them.

Now, I know it sounds a little odd, but I'm telling you this was a stroke of genius on my part. I got a book out of the library, a very simple, easy-to-comprehend book on making explosives. And I did. I spent the next two weeks, every single solitary day, creating what I hoped would be a very small, but effective, explosive. I talked to Frieda maybe once or twice during this time. She actually wanted to get together with me, but I was consumed with this. I knew that after I had completed this final confrontation, then I would be able to abandon *all* my fears: I would be able to start the job, take public transportation, fly. Hell, I'd even be able to take a ride on a ferris wheel.

I made the reservation the day before the flight. A commuter trip to Washington and back. Bingo, easy. Usually as soon as I make the reservation, I get stomach pains, but this time—nothing. I slept like a baby the night before, without any drugs, and when I got up in the morning, the familiar dread of flying was not there. I actually looked forward to the trip.

I knew that fifteen minutes after the eleven o'clock flight took off, something was going to go wrong on the plane, something that may have no impact on our lives or may kill us all, and let me tell you, when you face death, look it in the eye as I have, then you understand life in a very different way.

The morning was clear, not a cloud in the sky. I was wearing my Chanel suit, a gray one with black specks, very chic, very understated. I looked divine. I wore Chanel No.5 because I thought it would round off the attire, and the scent has always been good on me. I had been waxed the day before and had a fabulous manicure and pedicure. The gal who waxed me told me that I had the best set of legs she'd ever seen. Not a speck of cellulite.

I had placed the device in a book, *Valley Of The Dolls*. I thought that was somehow fitting. I had carved out the innards of the book and put it in a suitcase with some crumpled newspaper. It was a little satchel, a nondescript thing, and I sent it through the baggage claim, because I knew I couldn't get it past the x-ray machine.

There was a delay, but I had accounted for that, because if you've flown three times you know they all lie about departure time and figure it in to their arrival time. That way they can say they have the best on-time record in the industry. Such bullshit. Anyway, I was beginning to get a little nervous because it was taking longer than even I had anticipated. Finally, we started to take off. We were on the runway and it happened. I couldn't believe it. I was sitting there, perfectly calm, and the thing I had made, this stupid little creation that I had thrown together with this and that, me, a science dud, it worked.

People were going crazy. At first there was this stunned silence because no one really knew what was happening, but the next thing we knew, the plane started skidding and then it tipped over onto its side. The side I was sitting on. I have to admit, the explosion was more intense that I'd expected, but I had used extra explosives. I tend to lean toward excess, I always have.

At first there was no fire, just black smoke filling the cabin. The oxygen masks fell, and some people did what they were instructed to do. Most people just panicked.

I didn't. I couldn't believe it. I sat there, calm as a cucumber. I didn't know what was going to happen. I didn't know if I would live or die, if we would all expire in flames or if this was more show than anything else. I didn't know and yet I was calm.

And then something went wrong with the exit door closest to me. Everyone had to turn and use the door closer to the front of the plane. I was still sitting there, and that's when I saw the little boy. He couldn't have been more than four, cute as a button, and not the least bit frightened. He was amazing, he seemed completely calm. Whoever he was with was calling out his name, but by then the black smoke really started to get thick. I jumped out of my seat and went to grab for him, but there was a mass of people pushing from the back of the plane and he went down. I saw him, I saw him actually fall under everyone's feet.

TO BE CONTINUED...

THE PEARL FISHERS

LINDA NELSON

> *No ill-being, no cause of ill-being,*
> *No end of ill-being and no path;*
> *No understanding, no attainment.*
> —from *The Prajnaparamita*

THE MEETING, 1995

HeLen

I lower my head back onto the couch. I move very slowly, the way syrup pours on a morning when snow remains patchy on the ground, slowly so as not to spill the liquid from my ears. The liquid is brainmelt. You first drink the hot burning cocktail, and then your brain liquefies. It's a wonderful thing. A wonderful wonderful thing.

Must not spill onto the couch. Must not let my head tilt so that the melt sloshes over the rounded, twisted dykes of my ears. Don't want to stain the couch, don't want her to know I am about to spill everything she has given me: the grammars, the Dickens, the secrets, the Yeats. The scotch.

I can hear her in the kitchen. She is talking to the cats. The refrigerator opens, closes. Three cubes clink clink clink. Fork into the sink. Soon she will be coming back. I can smell the damp, dark tuna smell. Click click click, cheap white sandals against linoleum.

"You know, Helen, I don't understand what Philip sees in Kirsten. Do you?"

I keep my eyes focused on the ceiling. I don't need to look to see the long hook of Ava's nose, her thin lips carefully set, the rosy lipstick unevenly worn after a day of teaching. I don't have to see her because I know she is going to sit beside me on the couch and then she does and I feel her sleeve brush my arm. With my head tilted heavy back her smell wafts up my nose: stale lipstick, tattered hairspray, burnt toast. Cat food. Some kind of powder. Chalk dust.

"Are you sleeping, Helen?" The mysterious burr of her voice. The accent, supposedly Viennese, stretched out the vowels of sleep as if she longed to analyze me. She is either a refugee from the Nazis or she is not. She was raised by nuns in London, or maybe by an older sister here in the States. She might not have a sister. She was the first person I told. Ignoring the warnings of friends who had told me she would try to cure me, denying the whispers of others.

No, not sleeping, but maybe dreaming. The TV flickers on. I watch its shadows on the ceiling, its blue rays bouncing off the flat black glass of the picture window. The house gazes across a dead-end street toward empty lots and neighboring houses, whose only difference from hers is color. Her grey Chevy Nova with its plush red interior is in the drive; I'd come with her straight from school, and so must stay until my parents can drive the half hour tomorrow morning to pick me up. She never draws the drapes. If there is anyone out there, she wants them to see us sitting on her couch together.

I don't dare tilt my head. She would be furious if I stain the couch, but more furious at my inability to hold her Chivas, and much more furious at my failure to keep up with and confide in her. I can't look at her. Where would I be without her? Everything is louder than it should be; my world a Cage symphony of

X's, hand claps, pencils beating on black metal music stands. The deep, full sound of her briefcase latches being sprung. It sits on the coffee table before us, guts exposed, the red razor points she uses to grade our papers rising from it like jagged teeth. A buddha box.

"I want you to read this," I hear her say, but her voice is fading into a televised distance. I'm floating in this blueness as if I've left the cul-de-sac and floated off the earth's horizon, right there, into that deep midnight blue stain of setting sun, the same blue as the brainmelt inside my skull. The blue liquid hums with energy and perfect pitch, but through it I can hear the echo of the oboe, the long whining of the strings, the tympani being tenderly touched. The orchestra is warming up.

JACK

From the moment I entered to the clear burr of the oboe's A, there was no doubt the blonde woman was flirting with me.

She'd been leaning over the balustrade when I approached, her smooth-skinned back stretched across the easel of her shoulder blades. A sleeveless blouse of a glistening, lightly iridescent material complemented the fine, nearly white helmet of her closely cropped hair. The entire effect seemed to have been chosen as if to reflect the evening's performance of Bizet's "Pearl Fishers."

I stood for a moment at the entrance to our shared box, blinking down upon her glowing backside. The shimmering orbs of the stage lights and the too-polite murmur of those tucking themselves into their orchestra seats crested her sorbet shoulders and worked their way toward me like a warming mist.

Though I hide it well, this is not my natural milieu. New York's Lincoln Center is to Los Angeles' Los Feliz district as Kathleen Battle is to Nona Hendryx. But Los Feliz is long ago and far away—the car, the boys, the tree. Freya and John. And the desert between there and here was wide, the car I drove across it slow. I've had twenty-eight years to re-create myself. Like a lucky Rod

Serling character I have stretched and refined my features, my voice, my language, so that the tough street chica I was no longer exists. Each evolution of myself lives now like one of many textured layers beneath my smooth surface.

I was standing like this, hands deeply in my pockets with my fingers wrapped lovingly around my car keys, ready to turn and leave—to forsake the night's culture as I should have originally when the client I had planned to entertain had canceled—when she turned her head. Not all the way around to look at me, but halfway, as if she had caught the smallest hint of my scent. Her right cheek faced me, its small-boned delicacy seeming to reach toward me with the softness of sweet pea tendrils in a spring garden.

As if there had been no pause—deliberately, I later thought, so that I might study her perfect countenance, as if this entire scene had been produced knowing I would come through that one door to her box—she finally turned to look at me. Her eyes were wide and of a color I, caught within the bronzeness of the concert hall's decor, could not immediately identify. She wore light gold-rimmed glasses.

She parted her lips in a practiced smile and stood, extending her hand as she stepped to greet me. Her head tilted slightly, giving her a quizzical look, and I sensed again that she was sniffing the air and seeing the wolf beneath my fine suit.

"I'm Helen," she said.

HeLen

On our third date we met at Le Figaro for coffee.

I was still taking off my hat when Jack said, "There are only two kinds of relationships, you know. The first is the kind where you have known someone for years and come to adore them. Then, although they are most often not your type, you adore them so much that it simply doesn't make sense not to have sex with them."

I pulled out my chair and sat down at the small cafe table. Outside, Bleecker Street was much quieter than I remembered. Since moving to Third and 86th, I rarely get downtown. I slowly shifted my eyes back to his face. Had I ever seen anyone quite so lovely? Could anyone quite so lovely actually be attracted to me?

"The second kind is much more common," Jack said, lowering his eyes and stirring a spoon with feigned idleness in his coffee. He paused, looking out the glass window at the street. His nose was large and aquiline, his hair coarse-looking and sliced into jagged spikes around his face, so black it shone purple—not like a bruise but like the robe of a make-believe king. The entire effect was exquisitely foreign—Greek? Roman? Romanian?

The silence ticked against my nerves and I tried to imagine what he was thinking as he consulted the swirling text of bodies on the other side of the glass. Had he chosen this place as a psychic might, to read the runes? It was such an old-fashioned, and now tourist-infested, haunt. Perhaps in the yellowed newspapers curling from the walls he imagined the ghosts of Kerouac and Ginsberg still prevailed, and that I would find this excursion into the center of the old Village romantic.

Jack's appearance more than two weeks ago in my box at the philharmonic had shaken me out of one of my horrible childhood fugues. They'd become more frequent in the last few months and I was scared, feeling ever more powerless within their grasp. I didn't want to return to that time, yet since I'd left D. it was as if my life had been broken over my head like a china bowl. Bending over to pick up the shards was making me dizzy and nauseous.

The night Jack had appeared I'd been leaning over the railing at Avery Fisher Hall, trying to soak up the atmosphere of beautiful people parading below me to their seats, as if I could, by proximity, experience a kind of normalcy I thought they had: low shrubbery and multistory houses in Westchester, credit cards in a husband's name, children to whom they could justifiably dedicate their attention. All the things my parents had expected me to have. People with nothing left to accomplish.

But I'd had Ava.

"The second kind," he slid his eyes back toward me until I was caught in their wide judgmental gaze, "is when you simply must have sex with someone. You must have them. You are filled with what you imagine is the person's smell, their taste. You become feverish and do not know where you are, you immediately imagine the home you will make together. It is like a sickness. But in this type of relationship you shall never know the other."

I was being given a choice. As resounding as a slap, for I had never been offered such a thing before.

And, in fact, I wasn't being offered it now. There never is a choice in this situation, and indeed that was exactly what Jack intended. One does not choose relationship type number two. It happens to one.

If one is lucky.

Jack

There was no hint in any of those first meetings of what was to follow.

Helen was a witty and charming companion, smiling radiantly at the orchestra's performance, clapping her palms together flatly with the exuberance of a misplaced child. I watched her to know the proper places we might later discuss: catching for the first time some of the meaning in the wild swings of the conductor's arms; noticing, because she leaned forward, when he would bend into the wind section like a tree wanting to topple in a storm to cue in a particular musician. Each one received such special attention.

Usually at such events I allowed my attention to drift from whichever client I was escorting to survey the crowd, to calculate how I might best capitalize on their desires. The people who attend the philharmonic are like foreigners to me. My job, the role I had devised and crafted for myself after years of cursing in restaurant kitchens, is to facilitate the dreams of the women who hire me. Yet I've never pretended to understand why their dreams tended to overheated concert halls and sequined gowns.

Helen later told me she had been a clarinet player in her youth; from then on I studied and probed her mouth for a hint of the buck teeth she worried the single reed mouthpiece had caused. Yet, of the two of us, I think I remain the better performer. She has steadfastly refused to enter such competitions.

But that first night—when ordinarily I might have slipped from present fantasies into the past and again been confronted by that one, most fateful night of my youth—Helen allowed her bare shoulder to brush the fine wool of my jacket. I placed my elbow on our shared armrest and inclined my head toward her ear, eager to lie to her, eager to draw her closer.

Before I could speak, however, she surprised me. She didn't turn toward my lips but away, so as to continue to stare straight down to where the members of the orchestra were coming back on stage in that strangely discordant manner they have, pushing each other's chairs and music stands and veering through an arbitrary maze as if they never spoke to each other. By the time they were all seated, the stage seemed oddly askew. Helen glanced at me out of the corner of her eye.

"You've never played, have you?" she said, and she shifted away from me.

I could feel her tendrils loop and tighten around my throat, causing the blood to thicken in my chest, as if the cauldron of my heart had boiled over and, having no other vent, the molten fluid rushed upward through each available artery in a perfect volcanic spume. My face darkened with the admission of all I suspected she had discovered; she had seen through my fancy jacket and fine shoes and watch. She knew. But how much did she know?

The conductor emerged from the wings just as I began to speak. The applause drummed against my blood-tautened skin, drowning out the libretto I wished to impose upon this scene. The conductor raised his arms, seeming to arch up onto his toes in his desire to pull music through the crown of each musician's head. The applause subsided.

I knew that I, like others before me, would take Helen home despite the consequences.

THE TRIP, 1967

Jack

Lightning flashed dimly, distant. I was driving east through the Texas panhandle; fast, putting as much distance between myself and Los Angeles as I could. And I had never seen anything like this: the sky boiling dark and angry over the road, the world reduced to a black tunnel of water all around me, cold water which quickly began to seep through the floorboards of my '66 Bel Air. I pulled the car into a lonely diner, nosing its engine toward the tin wall. Switched off the ignition, left the radio on. Reluctance scratched against the inside of my bones as if my remaining strength were being chiseled away.

I rested my forehead against the cold, unforgiving plastic of the steering wheel, and the images were so vivid it was as if a week had not passed since my departure, as if I had not been driving blindly through red and yellow and painted deserts in a kind of madness for all those days. There it was, still spread out beneath me: the entire San Fernando valley sparkling with the vivacity of knife points. I was hanging upside down against the trunk of a tall oak, full of acid and laughter and fearlessness, and now I remembered wondering: is this what god sees? Or hawks?

In that moment I knew irrevocably the priests had lied: if this were god's vision, then I was god. We all were our own gods. I was most certainly god, born a foundling of Catholic Charities in Middlesex Hospital a mere ten blocks from the cemetery in whose trees I now cavorted. The hospital in which my daughter, too, had been born two years ago.

That night in the tree, and Freya in the next one over, the acid was old, not that good. I'd had a tab and a half—a pale blue turning yellow becoming brown, like sugar dots on a piece of wax paper. Someone's home brew, I knew, because I was still aware, absolutely, that I was in this tree, in this cemetery, in this country. I still knew, damn it, that I could not fly. This was one of the great moral fables of my youth: LSD had caused variety show host Art Linkletter's daughter Susan to jump from a window, flapping her arms, and fall to her death on a New York City street. My parents tried to use Susan to warn us that drugs only destroyed, but we were dying to be ruined by the vision of god. My god of razor thin eyebrows and curling lips and a voice between a whisper and a rusty hasp, making fun of people from behind his Oscar Wilde cravat on his Hollywood hillside.

The god I would become. Even hallucinogens could not break the suction my mind had upon my future. I knew my enemy early on: that twisted underworld of fantasies, demands, ambitions, and fears that had made me, despite the confessional, love to fuck; that had prevented me from using birth control and had kept me shy of the abortionist; that requires me, even now, to awaken to a new me every day.

That night, however, that night up in the tree, surveying my hunting grounds, that night my wallet fell from the back pocket of my jeans. I'd lost weight and hadn't noticed. It took a long time before I heard the soft thud as it landed in a loose pile of dust and eucalyptus bark at the tree's base.

This is how things happen. John, with whom Freya had hiked the Pacific Rim Trail, John who had proposed to Freya and who had been rejected after Freya hooked up with me, John came looking for Freya that night. And as my wallet flip-flopped slowly toward the waiting compost, a car appeared as if shot from the sky. An Asteroid. Its windows rolled wide, the persistent driving intercourse of an electric bass and the as yet uncut, untested sound of boys' voices slamming forth.

But now I got out of my car in Texas, reached back in to turn off the lights, swayed toward the door of the diner. In those days I had a ritual question for women I'd meet, and the waitress, her flesh clinging whitely to a visibly crumbling armature, was no exception. Will you come with me? I waited. I had no exceptions. I was nineteen and nothing—neither mutilated bodies nor my frantic flight east across the country—could disturb the myths in which I shrouded myself. I believed in these rituals: seduction, abduction, rescue, escape.

The music tunneling from the car that night in the cemetery was what I'd grown up with: Mexican, all shiny brass and circular rhythms made to flare a girl's skirts. I could feel my hips shift against the tree limbs. It was a horrible coincidence, of the type that occurs all too frequently, that the car had pulled up just as John had reached the top of the hill on foot. John had come looking for his girlfriend Freya, who had brought me acid in hopes of moving into my room at the YWCA.

Girls like that just seem to find me.

The oak leaves do change color in the foothills of the San Gabriel Mountains. Standing in the entrance of that Texas diner, the rain a solid sheet behind me, I still felt the pure joy of the tree's wide arms cradling me. But then the Asteroid had thundered to its place beneath my perch, snorting and belching. And rising from behind the vehicle's roof like a renegade moon, his curly blond hair bushy and lit by the car's lamps, John.

He walked right up to the car as if it weren't there, so naive in his whiteness. I watched a beer can fly from a window, heard a torn laugh.

"I know you're up there," John yelled in his clear beautiful tenor. "They told me. Dykes!"

"There's no one up there blond-boy, what are you doing here?" The car itself seemed to answer him. I heard Freya move worriedly in the other tree.

"No!" I hissed.

If John hadn't come along that night, I might have listened to my wallet fall, knowing it was too dark for the *chollos* to find it. Freya and I could have giggled and hushed each other without them knowing a thing. And only the tree would have had initials carved into its skin. And I would not be running from that beautiful cemetery.

Now here I was, seeking refuge from a deluge in a diner. Shifting one side of my mouth in a manner I had long practiced, I gave the woman across the counter my most disarming smile, studying her hearing, longing to offer her red, deep red. Yearning to lick color back into her skin, to refasten it to the tissue beneath. But this waitress wasn't interested.

I didn't really know where I was headed. Only away. I ordered hash with extra potatoes and hot sauce. Oval racks of postcards formed a semi-screen between me and the two guys seated bulky shoulder to bulky shoulder at the other end of the counter. It was still dark, that moment before the sun glances off the earth's most eastern edge to explode above us. I could see the guys' trucks like dark shadows through the rain. Their hair was freshly washed and neatly parted, their coffee slopped across the Formica in front of them. I could feel one of them wanting to whistle. Not quite sure.

I tried to bring myself back to reality by wondering where along these routes my brother, a truck driver himself who specialized in slipping migrant workers across the border, might be. Yet smelling the fatty, salted meat sizzling on the grill, the lights around me seemed to dim the way they often do at dawn, as if everything, man-made or natural, were deciding whether to go on one more day. I jerked myself back again, wondering how near or distant my pursuers were.

I forked a mouthful of hash into my mouth and wiped grease across my sleeve. I'd been forced into the desert. They had my wallet at the scene, they had my disappearance. No one would ever believe otherwise.

A low sound escaped through one man's teeth, and I couldn't take it anymore. Not the rain, not the week, not the memories, and definitely not this trucker staring at me. The slinky, spitty sound I thought I had heard made me waver: maybe I had done it. Maybe that steely smell on my hands was blood. The thought made my eyes burn with the desire to hurt this man, to teach him a lesson, to hear him cry out in fear.

Before I could think about it, I was upon him. The yellow-gray bristle of his double chin sickened me. My teeth clenched. Fury raced through my veins. There was nothing but this. I was behind him, and he was stunned and didn't move; there could be no resistance to my awesome, animal will. I bound the man's wrists between my long-fingered hands and dragged him into the parking lot before the waitress could reappear.

"Next time," I hissed, "don't even whistle for your dog." Then I played cat and mouse with a long razor I'd taken from one of my brother's friends back home. "So, how do you like it?" I shoved him down into the open trunk of my aqua Chevy; his watery eyes were wide, hair slick with sweat. "Is it as good as you imagined it would be?" I lightly scratched his cheek. His blood bubbled anxiously to the surface. "I think everyone should live their fantasies," I told him, and I laughed at the noxious gases he emitted.

I sliced his trousers into vertical strips and left them hanging from the belt at his waist. He opened his mouth but could not edge words around his thickened tongue. I lowered my eyelids at him, flirting.

"Why, don't you look sexy that way." I indicated his bare legs through the denim fringes. "What have you got under there, I wonder?"

His penis hung limp and gray, slightly blue-tinged with chill and fear like the day itself. The man's boots protruded from the high-slung rear of the Chevy. I leaned over, wishing I had a match. I tried to coax his balls with the razor to no avail. It takes most of us too long to realize what we are most often betrayed by.

A dull thud in the distance—thunder? the trunk lid slamming down?—caused my bones to shiver in disgust. The rain had stopped as quickly as it began. My feet were cold and damp, as if I had indeed been wading through puddles in the parking lot. I looked up at the clink of glass on china. She was standing there, the waitress, still pale in the post-storm dawn, with the coffeepot in her hand, staring at me. The palms of my hands felt seared, and I heard something drop. The waitress whirled. I knew just where she was headed.

TO BE CONTINUED...

SHADOW LINE

ELISABETH NONAS

I hated pulling the blinds but I had to. The Michael Best Clinic in West Hollywood was a modern contraption with floor-to-ceiling windows. These served a wonderful purpose in the clinic waiting rooms, brightening what were usually dark, dismal environments, but made the office a very difficult place for meeting with clients. The room looked out over Beverly Boulevard, and the commercial glare hit even three floors up. No matter how I arranged the seating, someone, either me or my client, would be backlit. Not conducive to productive therapy sessions.

So I slanted the mini-blinds to dim the light as best I could in a feeble attempt to emulate the neutral quiet of my private office. I volunteered at the clinic two mornings a week. When I wasn't in, other therapists used the space. We each had a few clients with regularly scheduled appointments, plus two or three walk-ins.

The woman who sat across from me now was a walk-in. I

learned only a little about her from her intake form. I didn't have the foggiest idea how Priscilla Townsend, age sixty-eight, from San Marino, the rich enclave next to Pasadena, had found her way to this AIDS Clinic in West Hollywood.

She was nondescript in a moneyed way. Not so beautiful she'd call attention to herself, but trim and well-groomed, well and expensively (Talbot's, no doubt) dressed in navy and white with accents of red. The effect was neat and crisp. Put her in any expensive neighborhood and she'd fit right in.

She looked out of place here, though, against the backdrop of the West Hollywood clones, the pierced and the muscled gymbots, and the androgynous punks who staffed and used the clinic.

I thought for sure this taste of West Hollywood was new to Priscilla Townsend. I guessed therapy was new to her, also. Years of being Priscilla Thornton Townsend had taught her to look poised in any situation, but her trembling hands and the shredded tissue she fingered gave her away. That and her inability to speak for a full five minutes after I ushered her into the office.

While I waited out her silence I tried to imagine the scenario that could have brought a San Marino matron to seek counseling services at this free clinic. I came up with: she had a gay son/ grandson who had AIDS and she couldn't talk to any of the girls at the club about it.

She cleared her throat once and I thought we might be on our way, but that didn't do it. The renewed silence made it possible to hear a little beeper chime faintly inside her purse.

She pulled a bottle of water from her bag, then a pill container—the kind I'd become familiar with. It had a built-in timer and ample room for a morning's supply of the drug cocktails so many people with AIDS had to take.

Priscilla Townsend could manage a healthy handful at a time. That took some practice.

Often I go on pure instinct. "How long have you been positive, Mrs. Townsend?"

She gave me a look filled with surprise and grief and relief and burst into tears. "I don't know." She shook her head. "I just seroconverted. My husband has been dead for two years."

"Who else knows?"

She shook her head again. "Except for my family doctor, I haven't told a soul."

"Didn't your doctor recommend—"

"He's been less than kind."

Seems that Edward Townsend, a banker, a good man, good provider, good father, philanthropist—I'd seen his name, their names, now that she mentioned it, on programs at the Music Center—this pillar of the community had kept a young man in West Hollywood for years. Never once mentioning this, any of it, until his first bout of pneumocystis.

"Edward conveniently went to Europe to die, so no one knew the cause."

I heard the slightest tint of anger in *conveniently* and had hope that I could dredge up more of the sludge buried beneath Priscilla Townsend's polite veneer.

"You said you have children?"

"Two sons. They're both in Northern California. I'm afraid to tell them. What if they refuse to let me see my grandchildren?"

"No one knows the cause of your husband's death?"

"Everyone thinks it happened on a business trip. My doctor intimated to me it was a good thing Edward was dead so he wouldn't have to know about my 'condition.'"

"So of course he didn't do anything like recommend a therapist."

She shook her head. "I thought I could do this alone. But I've been sick a few times."

"What did you do then?"

She gave a little laugh. "At my age, you're expected to get sick. No one questions the cause. Sometimes they assume it's grief over poor Edward." She dabbed at her eyes. "This is such a relief. You have no idea."

Even before her time was up she asked, "Could I make another appointment?"

Priscilla Townsend had more than enough money to cover my fee and felt bad taking up clinic time that would otherwise go to someone who couldn't afford to pay. We agreed to meet twice a week at my private office.

My next client, Madeline Baker, was already waiting. I'd been seeing her on and off for six months. She was in what I was trying to get her to acknowledge was an abusive relationship. "Lucky's just got a temper, that's all." Madeline had come in two weeks earlier with her right hand bandaged. "Burned it," she'd said. "Well, I tripped and caught my balance but fell against the stove. I'd just made tea, and the top burner was still hot."

The more elaborate the explanation, the harder an abuse victim was trying to cover up for her abuser.

I was pretty sure Lucky had shoved Madeline. She'd done it before, and Madeline wound up with a dislocated shoulder. The explanation that time was a real Rube Goldberg scenario that took five minutes to relate. I couldn't follow it all. The story became murkier with each of my attempts at clarification.

Madeline was pretty good about showing up when things were going smoothly with Lucky. When things were rocky, she'd skip our sessions. She'd missed last week.

Today she had barely settled in the chair before thrusting her hand out toward me. "Bandage came off."

"So I noticed."

"Practically all better, see?" She held the hand up, proof that things were okay at home.

I saw the pattern of the wound. Three curved bands on her palm and another set at the base of her fingers.

For some clients my expressions mirror what they consider appropriate feelings. Some aren't sure of the gravity of their situation until they see the concern in my face. Mirroring enables them to affirm that yes, they're really going through something big. Others see my concern and bolt.

Madeline saw me studying the burn pattern and self-consciously looked at it herself. "Cool, huh. I've got an electric stove." She extended the lines to complete a circle that looped back to her hand, the mark of the burner coil.

"Are you putting anything on it? It looks pretty tender."

"Hey, I already told you Lucky didn't do this to me, okay?"

We sparred for the rest of the session.

Talking to a victim of spousal abuse reminded me of talking to a brick wall. At least talking to a brick wall had the advantage of allowing me to imagine a dialogue. All I got here was more denial.

I had no other clients. I finished the paperwork required by the clinic and headed back to my private office. The billboards on Sunset screamed about recently released films, some of which my clients had worked on in one capacity or another.

I specialized in creativity. The bulk of my caseload consisted of people in the entertainment industry. I could help them with their frustrations because before I became a therapist I'd had my own brush with Hollywood and come out of it quite scathed.

I'd been in practice for almost ten years. But even the best of jobs can grow stale over time. The year before, I'd begun to feel my work was stagnating. I was no longer learning anything from my industry clients except what films were given a green light, what scripts were going into turnaround. Around pitch season I became a wealth of information (none of which I could share) about who was buying what. That wasn't what being a therapist meant to me, so I offered my services *pro bono* to the clinic.

In the year I'd volunteered at the clinic, I had done some of my most creative work. Still, I liked coming back to my own office.

It was tucked behind a gas station on Sunset. It had once been a private house. I owned the building with three other therapists. One retired recently but kept her office and showed up every so often to write what might be her memoirs, or a screenplay. The other two practiced here as well as out of their homes, so I was often the only one in the building.

A former client, a landscape architect, had bartered a trade with me for a rather large outstanding bill. She cleared her debt, and my colleagues and I got a Zen enclave adjacent to one of the glitziest streets in the world. From the utilitarian parking lot, heat shimmering off the asphalt, clients stepped into an inner courtyard hushed by plantings and falling water. Cool green and little surprises of color. A stand of bamboo.

I thought of it as a retreat. The whole space quiet and otherworldly. Shaded and dim. I was as comfortable there as in my own home. My small suite had its own shower and bath, which came in handy on the days I exercised before coming into work.

I'd decorated it in a mix of wood and leather, Japanese prints on the walls, shelves crowded with reference texts and self-help books. A style my best friend Peter derisively called early therapist soothing. Peter was an Academy Award-winning production designer. I couldn't expect to keep up.

My voicemail announced I had thirty-eight messages. Not possible. I had checked in the night before, as I always did before bed, and cleared everything. A quick call before I left for the clinic revealed only the usual. I had a successful practice, with its share of deeply disturbed people, but thirty-eight calls on a Monday morning was excessive. Even for me. This had to be a mistake, one I would have to deal with later, because my one o'clock was already waiting.

"Did you know the '63 Avanti was available with a 289 supercharged engine?" Oliver Pritchard was wearing a groove in the industrial carpet between the couch and the door. I'd learned in the two months we'd worked together that Oliver was a pacer. Today he sported the work clothes of L.A.'s *puer aeternis,* whether mid-twenties or sixties: tan slacks and a striped shirt, leather baseball jacket, loafers. Oliver was approaching forty, fighting like hell all the way. But that's not what had him all riled up. He'd just come from a meeting at a studio.

"Did you know it was the fastest production car that had ever been built in America? Aerodynamic design, built-in roll bar, caliper disc brakes. Way ahead of its time."

He sort of exhaled/spat the next: "You think I fucking care about Byron Benedict's goddamned '63 Avanti? I'm in there to pitch him my story—you know how many times he's canceled on me, or rescheduled?—and this is what I get. A detailed monologue on his fucking car!

"Asshole's last picture tanked, I've got just the story to save him, but all he cares about is this cherry set of wheels. We could see it from his office window. He spent my entire pitch staring at it."

I knew what was coming next.

"There's only two people in this town with any kind of integrity. Arnold Johnson and Michael Best."

Yes, the same Michael Best of the clinic. He ran his own production company. And record company. And who knew what else. One of the richest men in Hollywood, and its newest out gay man.

"And even then...Michael's the one who tossed me to Byron Benedict. That's supposed to be a favor? Now I'm going to have to pay him back for it, like when he calls me for a quick—meaning cheap—rewrite or a polish." He leaned back and closed his eyes. Oliver made his living, a handsome one, doing rewrites. "I'm sick of the fucking crumbs."

"How did the meeting ultimately go?"

He barely broke stride. "Oh, it went fine," he said in a tone that indicated just the opposite. "Everyone still loves my writing. On someone else's script. And they're still not buying mine."

He leaned back in the chair, exhausted. He closed his eyes. "Tell me again what the point of getting sober was? Nothing's fucking changed since Betty Ford."

Oliver had gotten into a bit of trouble in his drinking days. He was belligerent, sometimes rowdy. Mostly harmless, according to his own evaluation, but he had threatened a producer, resulting in a court order to stay off the set and away from the man. We'd been working on his temper, his rage at the system, trying to keep the focus on himself and off everyone else's success.

What would be the point of telling him a '63 Avanti was just a thirty-five-year-old car? I knew what he was going through. What a lot of my clients went through.

I'd had only one stroke of good fortune in my aborted Hollywood career, and it was many years ago. I sold a movie. Just a teen romance, but the idea was fresh, and my thinking was to give *Sweet Girl* a great soundtrack. By the time this picture was close to flying, I was no longer the biggest voice behind it: I was only the story's originator and along the line I got bumped. It went on to be a sleeper hit, the soundtrack an unqualified success. Michael Best had come in as producer and built his reputation on my film. I was furious at him at the time, though I knew there had been many other players between me and him. We'd never met. He probably didn't know I'd developed *Sweet Girl* from the start. After WGA arbitration, my name didn't even stay on as screenwriter, though I did get a shared story credit.

Therapy helped me. I ranted about Them and what They'd done to me, what They had and how They were keeping me from getting It. Whatever *It* was. When I realized I didn't know, I stopped and reevaluated. Once I understood that I thought It was some kind of happiness, not necessarily attached to fame and money, I had the great good sense to get out.

I went to graduate school and became a therapist. But I didn't leave L.A. I liked the palm trees. I liked the flowers and the smog and the Santa Anas. And now that I wasn't in the business, I could go to the movies or watch TV and enjoy it. I made a good living. I owned a house in West Hollywood.

And if my failure woke me in the middle of a rainy night, I could still enjoy the rain knowing the roof didn't leak. That if it did, I could afford to have it repaired. And I didn't have to see a therapist to debrief after every meeting with some Hollywood schmuck. That appellation courtesy of Oliver Pritchard, to whom I gave a few extra minutes because we'd been late starting, which meant I had no time between him and my next appointment to listen to my messages. Which now numbered forty-four. Clearly some snafu with the phone line.

My next client, Claire Johnson, came in brandishing the *Los Angeles Times*. "I was so excited to see you in the paper. Though I must say, it isn't the most flattering photograph." She studied it a moment. "I suppose it isn't a very recent one." She waved it in my direction. I barely got a glimpse before she yanked it back to read to me about myself. Or the paper's version of myself. "Let me see...." She searched and found: "'In a town where no one feels terribly secure about anything...,' that's not it, okay, here, '...therapist of choice to the stars, Zoe Albright. Albright, once in the business herself, traded in her computer for a therapist's couch. But her insider's take on the industry helped her build a practice devoted to fostering the creativity of above-and-below-the-line talent. Writers, producers, directors, actors, designers all sing her praises.'"

She placed the paper on the table between us. I caught another glance at my picture. The photograph was very old, and not that great when it was first shot. Still, it showed me in my optimistic youth, ready to take on the world since I'd clearly just about conquered Hollywood.

Nothing like having your failure stare you in the face. But at least I had a potential explanation for the phone calls.

"I'll leave this for you," Claire said. "We'll have a million copies—Arnold had his secretary buy a bunch."

With good reason. The headline blared PARADIGM SHIFT. The big news, the hot story to which the piece about me was a tiny sidebar, detailed the departure of Claire's husband Arnold Johnson from Stylus in order to form Paradigm, a new production company, with Michael Best. "'Industry insiders have been speculating for months that Michael Best, wunderkind producer, was looking for a new project,'" Claire read. She looked up at me. "They call forming a new production company a *project*? A project is a picture. A production company is not a project. It's much much bigger than that." She continued reading. "'Many were surprised today at his choice of Stylus chief Arnold Johnson. "I never thought Best would go with someone so studio-oriented," said one industry insider.'"

Claire had been hinting for months that something big was in the works. "I can't discuss this, even with you, though god knows it'd be safer talking in this room than in a booth at Nate 'n' Al's. Or even a car wash in this town."

Now that the story had broken she could talk freely. And she did for the rest of the session.

I heard all the hottest industry gossip from Claire, only it didn't come out as gossip: it was her life. They were going to this opening, or traveling to this location so Arnold could check on these movie stars. If she was having trouble with a friend, chances are that friend was someone I'd read about in the paper. Never much later than the week before. Despite a somewhat cultivated ditziness, Claire Johnson was sharp. She didn't have a job but she was not a trophy wife. She served on several boards, and not just in name, devising fund-raising and marketing strategies, managing PR campaigns.

Claire and Arnold Johnson inhabited the Hollywood ether, the galaxy of stars. Her husband and people like him were more powerful than the stars.

My next client was late, so I skimmed the paper Claire left for me.

Both Michael Best and Arnold Johnson were profiled. I looked at Best's piece first to see how much mention was made of his being gay. Quite a bit. The piece charted his history, including his taking over what started out as my project. And, something I hadn't known, Arnold Johnson had been associate producer on the picture. So this pairing was a reunion of sorts. Only now, a merging not of two promising young Turks, but of two of the most powerful people in Hollywood.

My photo came under a "where are they now" piece. Some therapists advertised their services and their specialties. I kept a very low profile. My shrink-to-the-stars listing probably was due to Kenny Gurwitz. He'd died of AIDS a few months earlier. Just before that, at the podium to receive his Emmy, weak and drawn and only a month away from death, Kenny thanked me in his acceptance speech.

I got a few calls from agents and producers after that. How about a story about a therapist who.... They wanted it for TV. For theatrical release. For cable. I turned them all down. But not without the tiniest spark of regret.

When Kenny talked about how I'd helped him with his writing, helped him integrate his life into his writing to turn out meaningful work, I wondered if maybe now, now that I'd been out of it long enough, learned as much as I had about the industry, and about myself, been away long enough to develop a thicker skin—

I stopped myself before I got in too deep. The pull of it was dangerous, seductive. Even after all these years.

Until *Sweet Girl,* I'd never failed at anything. And that had been a huge failure, public and humiliating. No matter that in any given year only a tiny fraction of the thousands of stories pitched for movies ever get written, much less sold. Much less made. No matter that, by virtue of *Sweet Girl* actually ending up on screen, even without my name, I'd done better than a lot of people in Hollywood.

Still, it hadn't been what I'd originally set out to do. And no matter how strong my recovery from that episode, how well I was able to maintain my house and my car and my lifestyle, under that substantial veneer I knew I had crapped out when I had wanted to score big.

The light indicating my client had arrived saved me from a deeper plunge into my dark places. And my client after that was right on time. I still hadn't played all my messages, but there was nothing I could do about it for another fifty minutes.

I tackled my voicemail while I ate a very late lunch. Most related in some way to the article: friends teasing, journalists calling for comments and follow-up. I skipped, for the moment, the reporters and obvious cranks, paid close attention to clients. One saying he'd be late, others needing to reschedule or to be called back. A doctor to whom I'd referred someone phoned to give me his assessment of the patient, completely professional and somber until the tag, "No business like show business, huh. Planning a comeback?"

Ethan had called next. After his hello, just a big sigh followed by "He fell. And there's something else, but I'll tell you when you get here. Will you bring dinner?" Ethan and Peter, my closest friends. Peter was dying, Ethan wouldn't get tested. Peter didn't leave the house anymore. We didn't know if it was a matter of weeks or days. I didn't, or tried not to, think about it. I just spent every minute I could with them.

Even only skimming the rest of my messages, I couldn't get through them all. Nor could I shake my dread of that "something else" Ethan had mentioned. I embarked on the rest of the afternoon grateful for my ability in times of stress to maintain close attention to detail.

My afternoon clients had read the paper, so we spent time dealing with the ramifications. Most people need their therapists to be inconspicuous. One man worried that now I'd have paparazzi hanging around in the parking lot. He was afraid of having his picture taken, of people knowing that he saw a shrink. "Pardon the expression," he added.

After hours of dealing with, dispelling, and allaying a range of fears and neuroses, including my own after the reminder of my failure, I was ready for something else. I stopped at home to feed the dog, who was singularly unimpressed by my mention in the paper, and headed off to shop for dinner.

I stood surveying the deli case at Chalet Gourmet. I took my responsibility seriously. As if food would keep Peter alive. So far I'd accumulated two different pasta salads and a cold chicken dish. Plus been greeted by my fellow shoppers and clerks because of the article, or just pointed at and whispered about. I kept my focus on the task in front of me, choosing vegetables and salad.

"Excuse me, Dr. Albright?"

Wishing I had just called out for Chinese to be delivered, and prepared to be gracious but brief, I steeled myself for another encounter. I turned to face a handsome young man. And I totally relaxed. "Guy, how are you?" Though I knew part of the answer had to be very well, since not a trace of the gauntness of addiction showed in his handsome face. His dreamy brown eyes were clear and bright.

"I'm terrific. I got a job, in production. And I met someone through work. And we're in a relationship."

"That's wonderful."

Guy Gutierrez had been one of my first clients at the clinic. A good-looking second-generation Mexican-American whose family had stuck by him when he came out but were baffled by his addiction. He'd come to me fresh from detox for crystal meth, West Hollywood's drug of choice. Crystal meth, as seductive as Hollywood, more dramatic, more deadly. He'd stolen for it, sold his mother's microwave, television, and a silver vase he'd once given her. That was the easy part, the part he told me about right away, in the first half hour of our first session. He talked about guilt and absolution, about making amends. He talked in a mixture of his own words and twelve-step catch phrases. Had no problem with this. It took a few weeks, twice a week, to get to the real stuff. The calls to 976 numbers, climbing a crystal meth phone tree until he found a trick in Laurel Canyon or Benedict or Nichols, once even as far as Studio City. Racing in his little Honda to wherever to do whatever to get his high.

Guy was into S/M, but on crystal he went way beyond serious play. He bottomed out the night he was almost killed by a guy he tricked with.

Guy had been my first client at the clinic. At least six months had passed since our last session, and clearly he'd done a fine job of maintaining his sobriety.

"I saw your picture in the paper," he said.

I wanted to roll my eyes but instead maintained a professional demeanor. "Well, don't believe everything you read."

"I don't. Especially in this case. That's my boyfriend they're writing about."

I must have looked stunned. Guy just nodded. "Right. Who could have imagined me and Michael Best. The best thing that ever happened to me." Guy laughed at his own little joke. Obviously one he told a lot, but I could see that he still was touched by it, and the corniness masked his genuine gratitude. "I mean, bottoming out was the best thing. And then the clinic—and that's pretty ironic, isn't it, that it should be his clinic. But he knows all about my past and isn't scared of it or anything and he's so great, don't believe everything you read, people in this town get so jealous. And...," he finally slowed a little, "well, we're just really happy."

"I'm really happy for you."

"Are you coming to the party?"

Michael Best was hosting a cocktail party to benefit the clinic. "If I can." I had actually planned to avoid it.

"Great. I can introduce you to Michael. I've told him all about you. He wants to thank you."

"For working at the clinic?"

"No, for giving him me." He blushed a little at that. "If I hadn't stayed clean, we'd never have gotten together."

We said good-bye, and I finished shopping.

My shoulders tensed as I drove up the hill to Peter and Ethan's. Even after these last few weeks of Peter's plummeting health, even after the last two years of a slow decline, I still had to brace myself for the shock of seeing a dying man instead of my friend.

TO BE CONTINUED...

DRAGON'S DAUGHTER

CECILIA TAN

This is a story that began in ancient times, so it is hard to know where to begin the telling. Perhaps at the beginning of the end, although even the end is a beginning, just as the end of the night is the start of the day, and the end of the day the start of the night.

Let us start then with sunset, with summer heat shimmering on the streets poured with copper light, as the fire eye of sun burned away a late-day thundercloud. Jin Jin stood in the window staring into the street, one hand holding the other against her fine silk dress. I start the tale here because it was the first time I saw her, placid and still like a statue brought from some dynastic museum and installed there as decoration for the restaurant. Which, in a way, I suppose was true.

I was rushing up the stairs, all sneakers and blue jeans, while Skinny Dou cursed in Cantonese and English from the bottom of the steps to hurry myself up. Imagine me, a bundle of sweaty energy bursting into that room, where the window burned with gold and she stood in cool silhouette, like an empress. The new world and the old colliding, my questions piled one atop the other: who was she, would I find clothes up here, why would no one explain anything to me, ever. Maybe Uncle Charlie would change his mind about this job. My mind was so busy, but my body went suddenly still when faced with her image and one last question: why did she stare out the window so, and for what or whom did she look?

And then the moment broke and she came toward me, speaking accented but understandable Mandarin. I could understand her! She said hello, asked if I was lost. I said hello back, but then couldn't find any more words. This is the ignominy of the American educational system: that to speak the tongue of my ancestors I had to fight to be enrolled in a special college class and trudge to it every morning at 8:00 A.M. I didn't think I knew the words to explain what I was doing there, anyway—how to explain the complicated relationship of favors and feelings and resentments that had led me to this, especially when I was only dimly aware of them myself.

My mother was thoroughly against my being here, embarrassed at the existence of the "restaurant" side of her family, as if somehow she was failing as an adoptive mother to keep me from falling back into the Mainland sordidness she thought she'd rescued me from. She and my father were both born in the States. My father's society brother, whose real brother was Skinny Dou, needed someone with good English and a Chinese face. Then there was my own insistence on providing for myself, a stubborn youthful rebellion in the only way I knew: I turned away the things my parents would give me in the same way I yearned to turn away their attitudes about all things Chinese. No, these things I could not articulate then. We exchanged names instead. Jin Jin Tsu, hers; Mary Yip, mine. But she could not say "Mary" and pronounced it "Mei" instead. So on that day, in that place, Mei is who I became.

Skinny Dou came into the room with his rapid-fire Cantonese, and Jin Jin herself was transformed from empress into seamstress in the instant she shooed him out and opened the wardrobe. As the sun dipped below the horizon, the glare turned to glow and I could see the room clearly. It was full of dark furniture, much of it lacquered wood upholstered with faded silk, chairs with carved feet and small tables at the edges of the room, a larger table in the center where four people could sit, and a surprisingly mundane-looking single bed pushed against the far corner wall, its white-and-yellow flowered bedspread looking like it could have been stolen from a cheap motel in Illinois. Maybe it was.

From the wardrobe Jin Jin pulled dress after dress, some large, some small, and held them up one by one, measuring them and me in a quick glance. She handed me a blue, high-collared *chongsam* and urged me with gestures and a few rapid words to try it. My eyes flicked to the doorway through which Skinny Dou could charge at any moment, but that was another thing I could not yet express in my textbook vocabulary. I could talk about baby things—pencil and car and tree and food, mother and father and brother and sister, house and shoe and cat and dog. But I had no words yet for worry or conflict or secret or dream. And so I changed my clothes, there in the middle of Jin Jin's room, while she hung up the unneeded dresses. No one came through the door. And once I was dressed, and the loose button at the shoulder mended, and my hair tamed and shaped into a compact bun held in place by two black lacquered sticks with tiny dragons on the ends, Skinny Dou came back. We easily heard his heavy footsteps on the stairs (for he was not at all skinny, no matter what his name) and his bellowing about how he would only pay me half for the night if I did not hurry. And then he opened the door and saw us, two little empresses, and he gave a nod and went back down.

Thus began my first evening working in the bar, trying to milk as much money as possible out of white men who had crossed the line from the financial district or downtown for cheap drinks and deep-fried dumplings. It was not, technically speaking, a hard job. My title was hostess—not really a waitress, not really a bartender, but something of both and more. What made it hard was my unfamiliarity with the workings of the restaurant, and the seeming unwillingness of any of the cooks or waiters to aid me in learning about it.

At the slow point of the evening, just before midnight when the dinner crowd was gone but before the late-night crowd came in, everyone ate dinner. Cooks and busboys in stained whites emerged from the kitchen and joined waiters in ill-fitting bowties at a round table in the back. Some sat while others ate standing up, sitting as soon as another would leave, all of them digging in hand-sized bowls of rice with chopsticks and chattering on about what I couldn't be sure. They were probably talking about me, from the looks and occasional words I could guess at. Too put off to vie for a seat, but not too timid to do something about it, I took a plate of greens and stir-fried fish and two bowls of rice and a pair of chopsticks in my hands, and before any of them could quite figure what comment to make, I marched upstairs to Jin Jin's room.

So, you see, that night was the beginning of many things, my first quiet meal with her, the first time she told me a story, the first time I earned money that my mother did not approve of, my first step into a world of Chinese Americans that was so unlike the one of violin lessons and tennis that I had known. I could not have guessed how far it would take me, at that time my mind on graduation a year away, with decisions to be made all too soon about careers and where to live and other things I did not yet know. Things that were easy enough to forget once I went up the stairs to Jin Jin's room, where she made me look proper, she said.

Every night I came upstairs to find her watching the sunset, even in winter when gray flakes clouded the sky. And we would sit at the *mah-jongg* table (for that's what that little table was, of course), her East, me South, sharing *siao bao* and trading stories. I decided not to start taking the Mandarin class again in the fall, not when I was spending late nights in her room listening to fairy tales and rhymes meant for children's ears, only now I was the child again, learning anew. She insisted that I tell her stories, too, as she learned English a word at a time, urging me on like an empress to an ambassador from a strange and faraway place. I traded her "The Old Woman Who Lived in a Shoe" for the tale of seven brothers who all looked alike and fooled an evil emperor who thought that it was but one man coming back again and again.

But now it is me that comes back again, looking the same, but never the same again.

I should tell you of another first, the first night I knew there was more to fairy tales than whimsy. I had always assumed that some of the stories she told me were made-up inventions, while others were based upon real people and events. I swapped "The Three Billy Goats Gruff" for the story of a fishseller to whom the Immortals gave a pill of life to keep his fish fresh. One day he swallowed it accidentally when hiding the pill from jealous rivals, and so became immortal himself. I told her the story of Cinderella when she told me of a pair of young lovers who cheated the gods. The gods banished the woman to the moon, and her sad face peers down forever at her lonely partner on the earth. And when it came to people who became legends, like Robin Hood and King Arthur, I heard the stories of a princess who became a warrior, of a scholar who saved the city from demons, of the emperor's concubine who became immortal. You cannot know what a treasure these stories were to me, whose mother had only told her Mother Goose and Hans Christian Andersen, and never the story of the seven lucky gods or of the dragon's daughter who could travel anywhere that the sky touched. But imagine me one evening, this maybe four months into my time at the restaurant, autumn air carrying the smell of hot oil over a crisp, cool breeze and night coming on early, climbing the steps above the dining room and finding the door to Jin Jin's room closed, locked. Through the door my ear detected a muffled, rhythmic sound.

I was naive, I suppose. Twenty-one years old, I was supposed to be a decadent American, raised on violent television and subliminal sexual advertising. But what did I really know? Some experimental fumbling with well-meaning boys, a passing knowledge of "stag" videotapes. It had never occurred to me to think why Jin Jin was there at the restaurant, whether she was a relative of Skinny (no, of course not, she would speak Cantonese then), or a boarder (where were her possessions? her pictures of home?), or what. Nor had I ever given a second thought to the Chinese men who often sat and drank tea with Skinny Dou at the back table, and sometimes went upstairs to play *mah-jongg*. If I had tried to consider it at that moment, I might have explained it to myself by saying that she had a suitor and that she was a wealthy renter who had no work. But maybe some things I had heard said that had not made sense at the time finally filtered in, or maybe I wasn't as naive as all that, because as Skinny Dou came up the stairs like a determined elephant, I knew that Jin Jin was not entertaining a suitor, and that she was not renting that room. How can this be possible, I was asking myself, that a man can keep a whore above his restaurant like it was the 1850s, here in America at the dawn of the twenty-first century? But no, I thought, as Skinny pushed me away from the door while hushing me with loud words, this is not America, this is not the same place and time. This is Chinatown.

I reeled back from Skinny, suddenly dizzy, as if I could not quite breathe. I clattered down the steps, not looking behind me, listening to the heavy clang of utensils against woks as I neared the kitchen, knowing that downstairs it would be as it had always been.

But it was not as it had always been. The room was bigger, a live fish tank bubbled in one corner, and familiar-looking yet unknown waiters stared at me as if I had just fallen out of the sky. Which, perhaps, I had. I must have come down the wrong set of stairs, I thought. Is this the place next door? I rushed out to the street to find the air warm, the breeze heavy with humidity, and the sun up in the sky. Not comprehending, not knowing, I sat down with my back against the warm concrete of an alley wall and hid my face in my sleeves, rocking back and forth like the released mental patients one sees in alleys in any city.

When I came to, I found myself looking into Jin Jin's eyes, stoic with Chinese concern. All was as before in the restaurant, as it had been every day I had worked there. That is, everything except Jin Jin's room, which I now saw in a different light. Jin Jin herself touched my cheek, but I could not, would not ask about what I now knew. We did not tell stories that night, I did not work at the bar, and I did not think I would return the next day.

But I did. In the morning I sat with my cornflakes, the TV on, in the kitchen I shared with three other students, and wondered once again what I was supposed to do with my life. Work in an office, make photocopies and type in a word processor? Build automobiles? My parents were both doctors, and I knew I did not want to be that. So what was left? Working as a hostess in a restaurant did not feel like a career, but it did feel better than not knowing. So many petty things are needed to make up a modern life: ATM card, traffic reports, touch-tone service. I could not eat the cornflakes. I felt terribly homesick suddenly, even though it was not my parents' home I thought of. I thought of the smell of frying dumplings and the clack of *mah-jongg* tiles punctuated with laughter as if remembered from an early morning dream. I could not sit there and worry about my diploma and resumés, when yesterday I had gone down a stairway and emerged in a sun-filled city somewhere else in the world.

I went to the restaurant in the afternoon, when I knew Skinny Dou would be sipping tea with his cronies at the teahouse down the street. Jin Jin was asleep, her black hair unbound from the dragon sticks and wrapped over one shoulder like a scarf. I found her clothed in simple cotton and lying atop the daisy bedspread. She sat up suddenly as I approached and rubbed her eyes, then smiled as she saw me. I had tried to guess her age so many times but could not. She had the eternal youth of Asians, I thought, always like we could be twenty, until suddenly one day we go gray and stoop, or get fat like Skinny. I said her name but could not form the question I wanted to ask—I was not even sure what it was I would ask. I tried to conjure the Mandarin words to describe something I was sure was real and yet thought could not be. Eventually I stuttered out, "Where did I go?"

She smiled again, her lips closed. Her hand over mine she answered, "China."

I laughed at first, until I saw she was not making a joke.

"You know now," she said.

I thought she referred to the fact that she was a whore, and I nodded.

"You can take me with you," she added.

And I, yes, still naive, still confused, and still trying to follow my heart, said, "Yes, yes of course."

So here is the danger of making promises when one does not know what one has promised. She was in motion then, braiding her hair into a queue, even as she crossed the room to the wardrobe. From the bottom drawer she brought out more clothes like the ones she wore now, unembroidered, of a sturdy blue cloth, with wide-legged pants and black slippers. I changed into what she gave me, not knowing why I was doing so, assuming that an explanation must be coming soon. Then, her hand pulling mine, we were tiptoeing down the stairs, and I began to think that perhaps I did not know where we were going after all, and that perhaps this was meant to be some sort of escape.

When Skinny Dou came in the front door and saw the two of us, and he shouted something that I could only guess was, "Stop where you are!" or, "Don't let them get away!" and Jin Jin pulled me at a run through the kitchen doors, then I knew it was an escape. Again I had that thought, this could not be happening, that a woman could be kept prisoner above a restaurant against her will, not today, not here…but mostly I was dodging the grabs of kitchen boys and then trying to see ahead of us in the narrow diagonal alley that ran between buildings. We weren't going to come out anywhere near my car, but maybe we would see a policeman, or we could run all the way into Downtown Crossing and take the train from there back to campus. In the alley there was the hiss of steam from other kitchens, the smell of rotten fish, and the sound of our slippers hitting the cobblestones. Jin Jin kept repeating, "Take me back, take me back," in a low urgent voice, even as we rushed away.

We emerged on the other side in a narrow, traffic-filled street, the sidewalk crowded with tourists. I pulled my hand from Jin Jin's and called for her to wait. I was out of breath, dizzy, and wanted a moment to think about details: car keys, visas, police. As the crowd moved around me, it felt like sometimes people suddenly changed directions and I was jostled. I pressed back against a wall and searched for her face.

Jin Jin was gone. People moved this way and that; cars crept slowly along. Across the way from me was a teahouse I had never seen before, with a red-lettered sign I could read in Chinese and English: GREAT FLOWER HOUSE OF TEA. The street sign was in Chinese and English as well, though it was clearly no Boston street: SANTIAGO. Not China either. Sweat trickled down my neck from fear and the air's heat. Inside the teahouse I found a newspaper that told me the answer: Manila, the Philippines. In a moment we had come halfway around the world, and in the confusion I had lost her.

They accept American money most places in Manila, and a dollar buys you all the tea you can drink. I sat down with a pot of jasmine and struggled to put my thoughts together. Why had I let go her hand? I had thought I was the one leading us but I was mistaken. My face looked round and brown and sad in the tea, like the woman in the moon. I had somehow opened the gates between places but had stopped short of finishing the journey. Where was Jin Jin now? Had I left her behind in Boston, to be caught by the cooks and returned to her prison? And how was I to get back there?

I suppose I could have gone to the U.S. embassy and told them who I was, but I could not bear the thought of my parents, of passports, of airlines and metal detectors. No. I had to be sure she was not here and not merely lost in the crowd. And if she was gone, I would find her, by what means I did not yet know.

I began to walk down to the main street, gaudy with red lanterns and the bright T-shirts of tourists, and up another alley. It ran alongside the back doors of laundries, bakeries, and butchers, whose doorways offered glimpses of brown-faced people, the scent of soap and fish and frying oil, but no Jin Jin. On another corner I watched two boys steal a mango, one distracting the shopkeeper with a sudden cry, the other hurrying past. Then they were both gone. The shopkeeper looked at his neat stacks of roots and leafy cabbage and fruit and frowned. Further down the row from him, two old women argued with a pharmacist, sending him up and down rows of hundreds of tiny drawers in search of the cure for what ailed them.

This could be happening anywhere, I thought, on any street in any Chinatown anywhere in the world.

As I turned to take in the scene I felt a breeze blow that I sensed was not from this place. Once again reality shifted. Around me, infinite gates with curved horns wormed away into the distance like a never-ending parade dragon. I held my breath, afraid to move and find myself in New York, or San Francisco, or I knew not where. And yet I knew I must take a step.

"Jin Jin," I whispered, and stepped through.

It would take lifetimes for me to describe all the things I saw on the journey, because lifetimes I did see—in cities across the world, in old Hong Kong and new Shanghai, in Chicago and Los Angeles, sometimes going back in years, sometimes going ahead—until I almost forgot that I was looking for Jin Jin. But never completely. I had come to understand that I must continue my quest for her, because I finally knew the answer to that question I had asked so long ago: *When she looked into the sunset, what did she hope to see?* Jin Jin searched the fire eye of the sun for someone to take her back to an older day, to a time when she was more than just a menu item, to when she had been the concubine to emperors. She looks into the lucky red sky for the dragon's daughter, and that is me.

Jin Jin is out there, in the vast timespace that is China, somewhere within the maze of kitchens and secret parlors that define it, and I will find her.

TO BE CONTINUED...

HUEVOS RANCHEROS

CARLA TRUJILLO

S ept. 19, 1968

Dear Grandma Flor,

Hi. How are you? Fine, we hope. Me and Corín are writing you this letter because we want to let you know what's been going on inside our house. Our dad, who we now call Eddie 'cause we disowned him, is still really mean. Eddie is living at our house again because our mom took him back, even though he never gave us any money to live on while he was gone and he had a girlfriend named Wanda, too. While Eddie was gone, our mom learned how to drive and got a job at Woolworth's. We didn't think she would take him back, but she did. Why? Who knows?

Eddie is mean. He hits us a lot and he lies to our mom about it. The other day he threw a pot of spaghetti against the wall that I was cooking for supper and then kicked and hit us so hard that I got a broken hand and Corín got a black eye that swelled up so big it closed. (She looked like the creature from the black lagoon.) Eddie keeps lying to our mom, saying it's me and Corín that's fighting and not him who's hitting us. Nobody (except our mom) believes Eddie, including Uncle Tommy who got in a fight with him and knocked him down with one punch!

We want to know if you can come out and help us. If you can't come out here to help us, please tell us what to do. Okay?

Thank you, Grandma. We will be waiting for your answer.

Love,

Marci and Corín

P.S. Don't tell our mom we sent you this letter.

We found a stamp in our mom's bills box and Grandma's address on the back of one of her birthday card envelopes that we always saved. We mailed it on Tuesday and in one week, we got a letter back from Grandma. This is what it said:

September 26, 1968

Mijítas,

I feel bad for you. I have to be hear for Tío Alphonso *porque* he is sick. He had un heart attack—not to bad, but he is fillin *mejor.* I think he gonna be fine. I am sending you money to take the bus to come hear and stay with me. Your mama is to crazy over your daddy and she no gonna leave him. So come hear and be with your gramma Flor and your Tío. I give you my phone number so you can call me when you get hear. We will come and get you. 505-555-7764

Love,

Gramma Flor

PS: *Mijítas,* don't take any shit from your daddy.

In the envelope were two twenty-dollar bills. We took Grandma Flor's letter and the money and hid them both between Corín's mattresses, way in the back where my mom wouldn't find them.

"What are we gonna to do?" Corín asked. We were sitting on the bed talking low, just in case Eddie or Mom came home from work early.

"I don't know," I said. "I don't want to move to Grandma Flor's unless we have to."

"Eddie ain't gonna change."

"I know, but I wish Mom would see what he's really like, so she can come with us."

"She won't."

"I know." I sighed really big and went over to my drawer and took out the knife that Grandma Flor had given me when she was here. It was four inches long and about an inch wide. It was a pretty knife, silver and black with a piece of turquoise in the middle. "Corín," I said, flipping open the knife. "Let's make Eddie change. Let's show him that we're not going take any shit from him anymore."

"Like how?" she asked.

"I don't know yet, but we can think of something." I looked at her and she looked at the knife. Then we smiled real big.

We did want to kill Eddie, if that's what you were thinking. God says not to kill, but it sure is hard to obey him with a father like Eddie. I wonder if God gave Moses those ten commandments for people who were in tough places like me and Corín, or were they just regular rules that he had to write to keep everybody in line? Who knows? Even though Sister Lizabeth seems to think she knows what God is thinking, I don't think she really does. I think she makes up most of what she says about God, just to get me to keep believing in him. Either that or she thinks I'm really dumb.

Probably the easiest thing we could have done about Eddie was just move to Gallup and live with Grandma Flor. But leaving your house and your friends, and your aunts, uncles, and cousins, is hard to do. Mostly, I think it was Grandma Flor's last words that made me and Corín want to do something about Eddie, even though we were scared to death to try. Grandma's tough. I know she doesn't take shit from anyone. You have to be that way if you raise a bunch of kids by yourself and run your own bar. Mom told me Grandma has a loaded shotgun behind the bar. She's fired it, too. Grandma says some men and even some ladies are mean as yard dogs when they get drunk. She doesn't mind it if they hurt themselves, but she sure don't like it if they start hurting other people or mess up her bar. No sir. Out comes the gun, and she tells them to get the hell out and don't come back unless they can act civilized.

Our grandma isn't scared of anyone. But me and Corín are just kids and we don't have Grandma or a gun. All we have is ourselves and our knives. So this is what we did.

We needed some help. We told Randy what happened and asked him to help us. Randy is a sissy, but he's also big and strong. We went over to his house after my hand got better and talked to him outside, on the front lawn where no one could hear us.

"You want me to help you tie up your dad?" He asked it like he couldn't believe it.

"Yeah. That's all though. You don't have to do anything else. You'll wear a mask so Eddie won't know who you are just in case he wakes up," I said, like it was as normal as buying a pack of M&Ms.

"I don't know, Marci. Your dad's way meaner than mine. I could get hurt or in big trouble."

"Randy," I took my finger and poked it in the grass, "don't be a chicken. Are you going to be a big chicken all your life?"

"Yeah—" Corín said it with a laugh before he could reply.

He looked at her, then said, "Probably."

"No you're not, Randy. This is your chance to stop being a chicken. All you have to do is get us some of that rope and duck tape your dad has in the garage and get your butt over to our house when we give you the signal. Our mom won't be home, so all you do is tell your mom you're coming over to watch TV."

"Come on, Randy," Corín added. "How do you think we feel? If we mess up then we have to pay the price and you know what that will be."

He looked like we were forcing him to jump off the Empire State Building.

"Randy," I said, "our dad won't hit you. He knows your dad would come over and kick his butt."

"Yeah, Randy. Your dad is lots bigger than ours."

"Mean, too," Randy admitted. His eyes were far away, thinking. "Okay. I'll do it." He looked at both me and Corín. "I'll get the rope and the duck tape, and help you tie him up. But that's all. I'm not going to do anything else."

"That's okay. That's all we want you to do," I said.

"And you can't tell anyone, not even the Johnsons next door," he added.

"Don't worry. We don't want them or anyone else to know either."

We all shook hands and made our plan.

We decided to do it when things were exactly right. That meant that our mom had to be gone for a long time and Eddie had to be drunk. What was good was that the two usually went together. Two weeks passed, and Eddie started drinking one day when he got home from work. Well, he always drank after he got home from work. But this time he started drinking a lot. Mom was working till nine o'clock that night, and Eddie was mad about it so he just kept drinking. He brought a six-pack home with him and I made a good supper of beans and chili. That way he'd at least be happy about the food. I didn't want him to have any extra reasons that night to hit us. I made the beans *guisados,* just the way he likes them, and I even tried to make tortillas, but they came out looking like the map of California. It made Eddie happy anyway.

"Mira," he said, as he shoveled beans and chili into his mouth with the tortilla. "This is the kind of *comida* you should always be cooking for your old man. Don't give me none of that damn wop shit you're always making. When you cook for your father,

and I am your father," he said, pointing to himself, "cook me some goddamn beans and chili. That's all I want. You hear me?" He turned to make sure I was listening. His words were fuzzy, so I knew he was already pretty drunk.

I nodded. Corín took one of my tortillas and heated it up on the *comal*. Then she spread butter over it, brought it to the table, and started eating it. Eddie watched her.

"Hey!" he yelled at Corín. She kept eating her tortilla and didn't even look at him. "Corín, goddammit, I'm talking to you."

"What?"

"Hey, those maps of Califas taste pretty damn good, don't they?" He started laughing.

"Uh-hmm. Yep, they're crooked, but good."

"Our little *hombrecito,* Marcito here, can cook pretty good, huh? Huh?"

Corín looked over at me. I hated it when he called me that.

"Oh, poor Marci." He saw he was making me mad. "What's the matta, *chiquito?*" He talked like I was a little baby. "You don't like it when I call you *hombrecito?* Well hell, that's what you are. I'm not gonna lie to you. Right? Right? Your daddy never lies." He started laughing again.

"My name is *Marcía.* Call me either that or Marci. Nothing else," I replied, my voice hard.

"*E'ste, mira,* Marci. Your mother and I made a big mistake when we named you. We should have called you Marcos. No? Marcos. *Pero,* how did we know you'd be a little boy when we saw your little *bizcocho?* We just went with what we saw." He took a long drink from his beer and slammed down the empty can on the table. "We didn't know no better."

I cut my eyes at him, but said nothing.

"Corín, get me another beer." Corín got up from the table, went to the refrigerator and got him a beer. He grabbed it, opened the can, and took another long drink.

"Ahhhh," he said, then burped. "But hey, I'm happy. I thought

I just had me two daughters, but instead I got me a daughter," he looked over at Corín, "and a son." He gave me a big fake smile. I gave him another dirty look.

"But I'll tell you one thing," he said, pointing at me, "you're gonna have to figure out sooner or later that you ain't never gonna be man enough to take on your father. Not as long as he's still standing. Hell no! Your daddy here's the one with the balls." He pointed to his birdy. "And he ain't scared of nothing. Nothing! You hear me? And I'm gonna tell you something else, he's got this big peter here to back up these *huevos* too. You, girl," he pointed at me, "ain't got shit down there except a little piece of tail. And that, little *hombre,*" he got up from his chair, "is all you'll ever have." He staggered over to the fridge and grabbed another beer. He took his half-drunk can and the new can and walked out of the kitchen.

"I'll show you someday how tough I am, you watch," I said. But I don't think he heard me. He walked into the living room and turned on the TV. Then he lay down on the couch and finished off the first can. He opened the second beer and started drinking it. In a few minutes he got up, turned off the TV, and went to the bedroom. I started cleaning up the dishes. After about five minutes I peeked into the bedroom while I was pretending to go to the bathroom and saw that he had fallen asleep.

"He's asleep," I said, returning with my hands curled into tight fists.

"Think we should do it?" Corín opened the fridge and saw that all six cans were gone. "He drank every one of 'em."

"Just a second. Let's go look again." We went back to the bedroom and looked at Eddie. He was snoring loud enough to wake the dead, as my mom would say. We went back to the kitchen to talk about it.

"I think we should do it," I said.

"Think so?"

"Yeah. Yeah, I do."

"Okay," she said. "Let's go then."

"I'll get Randy." Corín started toward the door.

I looked at the clock. It was 6:15. "No, wait! Not till 6:30. That's when they're done eating supper."

"All right."

We cleared and washed the dishes, and put away the food. At 6:30 Corín ran over to Randy's house.

In about ten minutes Randy and Corín showed up at the back door with rope and duck tape.

"I got the stuff, Marci," Randy said, breathing hard. His eyes were big and wide.

I looked at his red cheeks and his big *panza* as he tried to catch his breath. He held a bunch of rope in one hand and Corín had the role of duck tape in the other.

"Okay, Randy," I said, patting him on the back. "You did good."

I don't think I'd ever been that scared in my whole life. When we talked about it later, it seemed we must have been out of our minds. Maybe we were, cause that night something else inside of me was doing the thinking. I wouldn't be able to tell you what me and Corín were thinking about while we did it. And I don't know if she would either. When I saw the rope and tape, I didn't know if I could go through with it. But when I remembered what Eddie did to us, and how he said I could never stand up to him cause he's got big balls—even though Grandma Flor sure stood up to him and she's just a grandma—well, something about everything made me think I could.

Corín didn't waste any time. She got the rope we found in the garage. I got the scissors and cut some duck tape about as long as my hand. I stuck the piece of tape to my arm. We had our knives in our pockets and checked to make sure Randy was still ready to help us. He looked scared, but he didn't look like he was going to leak out on us. We told Randy to put the scarf he got from his mom around his mouth to hide his face. I thought it was going to be a regular scarf like Tonto sometimes wears on the *Lone Ranger,* but his mom didn't have anything regular, so the scarf was something kind of silky, like what you get from Montgomery Ward's. It was red with black and gold knots all over it. When he put it around his mouth, he looked like he should be in a harem instead of our house. I went into the living room and closed the drapes, even though it was still light out. We heard Eddie's loud snore coming from the bedroom. I peeked in on him again and saw his hands were over his chest. I gave the signal and we got our stuff and tiptoed into the bedroom. I motioned to Randy to kneel by Eddie's feet. Corín was on one side of the bed and I was on the other. I knelt down without making a sound, holding one end of the rope. Randy had another piece of rope. I looked up at the ceiling, hoped that God was watching, and gave the signal.

Grabbing one of Eddie's arms, I slowly wrapped the rope around his wrist. Then I took his other arm and, leaving just a couple of inches between his hands, I wrapped the rope around his other wrist. I was really nervous that he was going to wake up, but maybe God was watching, cause Eddie kept snoring. Then I gave Corín one end of the rope and I took the other and we tied each end to the front of the bed. Randy did the same thing with Eddie's feet. Randy was so nervous he was sweating all over his mom's scarf. He did good though. He moved carefully, lifting up each of Eddie's feet and tying the rope around them.

I finished tying my end of the rope that held Eddie's right hand to the bed's leg and checked on Randy. So far, Eddie stayed asleep and everything looked good. I couldn't believe he didn't wake up, but after drinking a whole six-pack, it didn't seem like he was going to be waking up for a while. After Eddie was all tied up, I motioned for Randy to leave. He stood up and snuck out of the bedroom. In the hallway he turned toward us and pulled off his mask. I gave him a thumbs-up, which I learned from watching *The Avengers*. Randy gave me a thumbs-up back and walked down the hallway and out the door.

Next, I peeled the duck tape off my arm and slowly lowered it over Eddie's snoring mouth. I knew he'd wake up as soon as his mouth was blocked so Corín went over to the other side of the bed and took her knife out. My knife was already on the floor by my feet. I checked the time on the bedroom clock. It was 7:05. I slapped the tape over Eddie's mouth. He woke up in a heartbeat.

His eyes got big and he tried to talk. All that came out of him, though, were words that we couldn't understand. But we had a pretty good idea what he was saying. He tried to pull his arms free but couldn't because we made the ropes really tight. Then he tried to move his legs, and when he saw that he couldn't move those either, he started getting mad. We could see it in his eyes. Nobody's eyes get as green and hard as his. Poor Eddie. We knew right then that he wanted to hit us real bad. But what was he going to do? He kept struggling, trying to loosen the ropes, but it wasn't going to do him any good, because this was a bed made a long time ago by one of my *tíos*. It was heavy and hard to move, which was why Tía Queta left it in the room when she moved out. Our knots were tight, too, which was about the only good thing we learned from Girl Scouts.

"No use struggling, Eddie," I said, checking all the knots and making sure they stayed tight.

"Yeah. It ain't going to do you any good to try to get loose. We got you tied up really good," Corín added.

"Mmmffhh, mmmmfffh mmmm!"

"What's he saying?" I asked Corín.

She raised her shoulders like she didn't know.

"He's trying to say something, I think." I looked at Corín.

"I guess he is," she replied. "Too bad we can't understand him."

"Yeah, too bad." I went up close to him. "Hey Eddie, do you want me to loosen the tape so you can talk?" I said it really nice-like.

He nodded his head fast, but his eyes looked like they wanted to kill me first.

"Think we should?" I said to Corín. Eddie looked over at her.

"Nuh-uh. Not yet. I don't want to hear him talk for a while. Let's go get some ice cream first. Mom bought some last night."

"Okay!"

We both got up and took our knives with us and walked out of the room. I could tell I was nervous because I was breathing kind of fast. I looked over at Corín and she looked at me. Our eyes got big like we couldn't believe we were doing this. We walked over to the fridge and sure enough, there was the "three-kinds" of ice cream in the freezer. Neapolitan. What a dumb name for ice cream. We were never allowed to have any treats like ice cream unless we asked. So it was fun to just walk up to the refrigerator, grab the ice cream box, and get our bowls like *we* were the bosses of our lives. After serving ourselves a big pile of ice cream, we walked back to the bedroom, sat on the floor, and started eating in front of Eddie.

"Maybe he wants some," I said.

"I don't know. He only likes the strawberry and vanilla part of this kind of ice cream, and I got mostly chocolate. What kind did you get?" Corín took a big spoon of it and shoved it in her mouth.

"Pretty much chocolate."

"Well let's give him some of that. He might like it anyway."

"I don't think Eddie likes chocolate very much."

"Yeah, he does. Let's give him some."

I took my knife and laid it next to the bed. Then I slowly lifted the tape off Eddie's mouth, but only part way.

"There, I think that's enough room to swallow a taste, don't you?"

Corín looked at the tape that was covering Eddie's mouth half-way.

"Mmm-hmm," she said as she shoved in another spoonful.

"Eeef yooouu keeds don't entie me, ahhmm goein tooo keek yurr leetle esses."

"Corín, I don't know about you, but I don't think I like the way Eddie is talking to us."

"Uh-uh. Me neither."

"Let's put the tape back on all the way. Sorry, Eddie. No ice cream for you. Maybe if you're nice to us, we'll let you have some. That is, if we have any left." I laughed. This was fun.

"I don't know, Marci. Do you think we should let him have any ice cream, since he doesn't look like he's going to be nice to us?"

"Mine's almost gone, so probably not."

Corín chuckled.

"Mmmmfffhh, mmmmfffh mmmm!" Eddie's eyes were hot coals. I was kinda scared because if he got loose, I knew he'd probably kill us. But right now, he couldn't kill a fly.

The sound of spoons scraping the bottoms of bowls was all the noise we could hear for the next few minutes. We finished our ice cream and set the bowls down. Eddie started struggling hard against the ropes. Corín looked scared, but seemed to feel better after I checked all the knots again. They were still holding tight, but to make sure, I tightened them.

"Let's wrap some tape around his hands and feet to really hold him tight," I said. "Corín, could you get me the tape and scissors?"

She brought me the tape. "Okay, hold the scissors ready. I'm going to wrap the tape around each arm and tape it to the bed. Eddie's eyes got even bigger and he tried as hard as he could to pull the ropes loose. Finally he stopped and lay on the bed breathing hard. "Looks like he'll be still for a minute."

I wrapped tape around his left wrist a few times, then brought it to the side of the bed. I wrapped it again, but brought it in the opposite direction so that his arm was held with a big V. I did this on his other arm, and then each leg. We were careful to make sure to rope and tape him above his work boots.

"I never knew duck tape was so strong, did you?" I asked Corín.

"Uh-uh."

Eddie was sweating a lot now. We glanced at the clock. It was 7:45. I looked over at Corín and nodded to her. We sat down on each side of him, close enough to smell his sweat.

"Eddie, we did this because we have to have a little talk with you," I said.

"Yeah, and we wanted you to hear us instead of hit us."

"We couldn't think of another way to do it, so sorry about all this." I raised my arms up, like I couldn't help any of it.

"Some of the things we wanted to say we've been wanting to tell you for a long time, but you never listened to us. And every time we tell Mom, she just believes you and not us."

"We just wanted to talk to you for a while, and if it looks like you're listening and will do what we say, then we'll let you go."

Eddie's eyes darted back and forth from Corín to me. He looked over at the clock to see what time it was.

"Corín, I don't think Eddie needs to see the clock."

"Good idea." She got the clock, unplugged it, and moved it to the floor, where she plugged it into another outlet so Eddie couldn't see it. "How's that?"

"Good." I turned my attention back to Eddie.

"Eddie," I said, speaking close to his face which was now looking up at the ceiling, "we have a few things we want you to do."

"We don't want very much, Daddy, I mean, Eddie. Plus, we think it will be easy for you to do what we want."

"Corín's right. What we want are just three little things. Ready, Corín?"

She pulled a piece of paper from her pocket and handed it to me.

"You want to read it?" I asked.

"No, you read it."

"Here's number one. You, Mr. Eddie Cruz, can never hit us again. Not with your hands, not with the belt, not with anything, no matter how much you want to, or how mad you get at us."

I looked at him. He still wasn't looking at us.

"Did you hear me?"

He nodded, then breathed hard through his nose.

"Number two. You, Eddie Cruz, can never call us names or say things to make us feel bad, or look stupid, even though that's what you might be thinking."

I looked at him again. He didn't give any sign that he heard me.

"Did you hear that one?"

He nodded again.

"Number three. You, Eddie Cruz, can never be mean anymore to anybody. That includes us, Mom, Uncle Tommy, Father Chacón, and especially Grandma Flor. You have to always be nice to us and them, even if you don't want to."

Eddie wasn't moving.

"Got that?"

He didn't move.

"I said, did you get that?"

He finally nodded, still breathing hard.

"Hey, Marci. I don't think he liked the last one. Let's ask him if he's going to do what we say."

"Now, Eddie, I'm going to pull this tape off your mouth. But if you yell, I'm going to slap it back on. Hear me?"

He nodded again.

"One peep out of you and I won't take it off for the rest of the night. Got it?"

Nothing.

"Okay?"

He nodded.

I slowly pulled the tape off his mouth. He licked his lips then started jabbering away.

"*A qué hoda!* You two little sons of bitches. I'm going to kick your little asses to Kingdom Come the second I get free. You better go live on the moon, 'cause that's where I'll go looking for you if you don't let me go right now."

"Marci, I told you he wouldn't listen to us."

"Cut me another piece of tape. That piece we had on him is getting kind of slimy." She cut another piece.

"*Hoditas!* You better let me go. I'm warning you!"

"What are you going to do, Eddie? Huh? Huh? Where are those balls of yours that you're always talking about now? They aren't helping you very much right now, are they? Are they?"

"If it wasn't for these *huevos,* you wouldn't be here today." He jerked his head in the direction of his balls. "Now show some respect for your father and cut me loose! Now! You hear me?! You guys got a lot of nerve doing this to your father. I'll tell you one thing, God is up in heaven and he's going to punish you for what you're doing to me."

"How?" Corín asked.

"He's going to make your hands dry up."

"Dry up?" Corín looked at her hands.

"That's right, dry up. They're going to shrivel up and waste away because you've struck your father."

"We didn't hit you," she said. "We just tied you up."

"It's the same thing. You're hurting your father and God's gonna punish you for it."

"When?" she asked.

"*A qué cabron!* How the hell do I know when it's supposed to happen? It's one of the ten commandments, *pendéja,* and you just broke it. God'll punish you. You wait and see!"

Corín looked at her hands again, then made them into tight fists. She opened and closed them a few more times.

"I don't know, looks like they're still working to me."

"You wait."

"I think he's talking a little too much, don't you?" She looked at me, still flexing her hands.

"Sure is." I took the tape and put it over his mouth again, which was hard cause he kept moving his head back and forth. Then he tried to bite me.

"Does God say anything about fathers biting daughters?" I asked.

"*Jotíto!*"

"There." I finally got the tape on his mouth. "Damn, Corín, I should have asked him what that meant before I put the tape back on." I rubbed the tape hard across his mouth to make sure it stuck. "Oh well, next time."

I picked up my knife and motioned for Corín to do the same. I rested the blade against his face. Eddie's eyes looked scared now, like he was about to get branded.

"We're not going to hurt you, Eddie. But you have to do what we say."

"Eddie, we want you to do what we asked you. It was just three things. But you know what, Corín?" I looked over at her. "I thought of another thing we should ask Eddie. We have to make him say that he's never going to kill us."

"That's right! How'd we forget that?" She turned back to him. "Okay, Eddie. We forgot to say you can never kill us. I can't believe we forgot that one!" she said, looking back at me.

"I guess we weren't thinking all the way. So Eddie," I looked at him hard, "you can't ever kill us."

"Or Mom, either."

"Or Mom, either. Got that, Eddie?"

He didn't move.

"Maybe we should show him we mean business, Corín."

We took our knives and slowly pulled the tips across each of his cheek bones, cutting a thin, fine line on both sides of his face. A small trickle of blood dripped from the cuts.

"Don't cut too deep yet, Corín."

"Mmmfffhh, mmmmfffh mmmm! mmmmfff! mm-mmm!"

"Eddie, do you think we like doing this? We're getting a little tired too. We just want you to do what we're asking, and so far you aren't showing us that you will." I sighed cause I was getting tired.

"Like we said, we aren't asking very much."

"Just do what we say. Eddie, are you going to do what we ask you?"

Eddie didn't move.

"Eddie, did you hear us?" I repeated.

He still didn't move.

I nodded at Corín. This time we took our knives and cut him across his throat. We made sure the cut was just light enough to bring some blood, but not too deep. We could do this because we had practiced on one of his old leather belts to make sure we knew how to cut light or deep.

Eddie got all excited again. He kept making all kinds of noise under that tape.

"Shut up, Eddie. I'm tired of hearing you piss and moan." It was fun saying his own words back to him.

I looked over at Corín. She looked really mad.

"Corín, do you think we're going to have to kill him?"

"I think we're going to have to, Marci. He doesn't want to do what we're asking."

Eddie started nodding his head up and down really fast. His eyes switched back and forth from one of us to the other.

"He looks scared," I said. "Maybe he will."

"Just because he's scared doesn't mean he's not going to hurt us," said Corín.

"Yeah. You're right. Let's get it over with." Eddie's face was so red it looked like his eyes were going to explode.

"We should cut his balls off first, though," Corín said.

"Good idea."

We moved from Eddie's face over to his pants. Eddie's eyes followed us. His chest was going in and out fast, with the breath coming out of his nose like a little train engine. He kept trying to talk. As we held the knives up over his *huevos,* I took another look at him. His hair was wet from sweat; his face was a bloody mess. And the white bedspread held little pools of blood from the cuts on his throat. He watched us raise our knives right above his zipper, then his eyes rolled up toward the ceiling and he passed out.

TO BE CONTINUED...

SKINNER AND CHOY

KITTY TSUI

Ching chong Chinaman
sitting on a fence,
Trying to make a shilling
out of five pence.

The ditty followed me everywhere. I couldn't escape it.

"Hey, chingy Slant Eye. Did ya eat bird's nests and fish heads today?" called the boy in a sing-song voice.

"No, she ate a puppy dog!" shouted another. "Yuck!"

"Your mum washes me mum's dirty knickers," chimed in a third.

"Your da' works at a Chinese restaurant. And 'e can't speak English."

"Ya eat chop suey with chopsticks and ya can't spell Wallasey. 'Cor blimey!"

My dad can too speak English, and I can too spell Wallasey, I wanted to shout. I know how to spell it very well, because I got it wrong once when the mayor was visiting our classroom and I had to write it out a hundred times after school. W-A-L-L-A-S-E-Y. *Wallasey, Wallasey, Wallasey* a hundred times. And no, my dad does not work at the Chinese restaurant. He's at see. That's what my mum told me anyway. I won't see him for months and then he's at home all the time. Then he'll leave again.

"Your dad's at sea," my mum says. Problem was, I didn't know what *at see* was.

"If anyone asks, tell them your father's at sea," my mum said to me one night.

"At see? What's that?"

But she wasn't listening. She had turned back to her knitting.

"All your friends have mums and dads at home, so we don't want anyone to think we're any different. You do have a dad and he goes to sea, but he's not an ordinary seaman; he's the second mate on board ship. So if your friends ask, say he's at sea."

"Eh!"

A harsh voice jolted me back to the present.

"Eh!" the boy shouted. "Got any pocket money? Let's 'ave it for toffee and comics and we'll let you alone."

"Come on then. 'Urry up!"

I looked at the boys. It was Peter Horner, the class bully, and his two pals, Nigel Payne and Barry Smith. Clutching my brown leather satchel closer to my body, I shook my head.

"What?" Peter Horner said. "Can't you understand plain English? Gimme that." And he lunged for my satchel.

I twisted suddenly so that his hand landed on my back.

"What the...?"

"Bleedin' chink!"

The three boys came at me as one and I suddenly wished I had money to give them. Arms flew at me and knocked me to the pavement, where I landed in a puddle of rainwater. While on the ground I saw in slow motion a skinny leg clad in navy blue knee-high socks and brown oxfords coming toward my face and I closed my eyes.

"Hey, Onion Head!" someone shouted. "Stop it! Stop that, you bully."

I waited, but miraculously the kick never contacted my body.

"It's Fatty Skinner," a boy's voice jeered. "Mind your own bloody business or you're next!"

The girl strode fearlessly to where I lay.

"I'm not afraid of you or your pals, Onion Head. Go on, scram!"

She placed her hands on her hips and glared at them. Amazingly enough, they ran.

"Are you all right?" she asked, holding out a hand to me.

"I think so," I said as I got to my feet. "Scraped my knees is all. Thanks ever so much for helping me."

"Don't mention it. My name's Alison Skinner. What's yours?"

"I'm Jean Choy," I stammered. I was not used to speaking with anyone other than my mother, and we spoke in Chinese. Well, I mean except at school, and that was only when I had to.

"Where do you live?"

"Uh...on Hillside Road."

"That's right by my house. Come on, then, I'll walk home with you."

"Oh, you don't have to, really."

I was grateful to her for rescuing me, but I didn't want to have to talk to her all the way home. I usually walked with a book held out in front of me. That was how the three boys had surprised me.

"Oh, come on," she persisted. "I'm going home the same way." Her face twisted in a grimace. "You don't like me, is that it then?"

"Gosh, no!" I shouted in dismay.

So she fell in step next to me as we walked along in silence. The autumn wind blew around us; I felt chilled in my wet clothes.

"I've seen you at school."

"Oh," I said.

"Does your dad work at the Chinese restaurant?"

"No," I replied with authority in my voice. "He's at see."

It was her turn to say, "Oh."

We continued on in silence.

It was almost dark when we got to my street.

"Good-bye," I said.

"Want to play sometime?"

"Play?" I ventured uncertainly.

"Yes, unless you like dolls, that is. 'Cos I don't. I hate dolls. We could go ride our bikes. Oh, do you have a bike? My dad's building me a go-cart. We could ride it down your street. It's a nice hill to go down."

I looked at Alison. She was a large girl, bigger than I, with fat red cheeks and a crooked grin. Her brown hair hung about her face like limp noodles. I imagined the two of us sitting astride her go-cart as it flew down Hillside Road.

"I hate dolls too, but I don't have a bike. I don't know how to ride one," I added in a small voice.

"It's easy. I can teach you."

"Super!" All of a sudden I did not want to stop talking and I certainly did not want to go home.

"What else do you like to play?" she asked.

I wasn't going to volunteer that I had a whole box of toy pots and pans and an elaborate tea set, and that one of my favorite things to do, other than reading, was to "cook."

"I like to climb trees and swing from high branches," she continued without giving me a chance to reply. "And I'm making a slingshot. Or at least I'm trying to copy the one that my big brother has."

"Wow! Could you show me too?"

"Sure, but only if you'll join my gang."

I was impressed. Alison had a gang.

"What kind of things does your gang do?"

"Exploring in the park, rock climbing, making up adventures. That sort of thing. Outdoor stuff. No watching cartoons on the telly."

"Oh." I wasn't about to tell her that we didn't own a telly and when I managed to get to a set, I liked watching cartoons. "That sounds like fun."

"Well then, want to join?"

"Who's in it?" I asked timidly.

"Well," she hesitated, "just me so far."

"What's the name of your gang?"

"Skinner's Gang."

"Oh."

"What's the matter? Don't you like the name?"

"Well, I..."

"What then?"

"There's just the two of us, right?"

"Well, right. For now."

"What about Skinner and Choy's Gang?"

I couldn't believe the words that had come out of my mouth.

"Too long!"

"Skinner and Choy then," I pressed.

"Skinner and Choy?"

"Yes."

She made a face.

"What's the matter?" I asked. "Why not?"

"It sounds, well, funny. Skinner and Choy," she chanted. "Skinner and Choy."

"Do you want me in your gang or not?" I said boldly.

"Well, there is one other rule."

"What is it?"

"Only tomboys allowed."

"Agreed. Skinner and Choy then?"

"Skinner and Choy," she laughed. "Skinner and Choy."

We joined forces as Skinner and Choy for the first time that very weekend.

It was Saturday morning, early. We walked to an area on the edge of the town that we kids knew as the Breck, sprawling acres of a no man's land, where tangled underbrush grew unchecked, and rusted tin cans and paper trash proliferated like wildflowers.

"Come on!" Skinner yelled as she spotted a favorite tree.

And she ran and clambered up its limbs, showing an unexpected nimbleness for such a large girl. I squinted my eyes and stared at her in amazement.

"Come on then! What're ya waitin' for?"

I hesitated, looking down at my feet.

"Gotta tie my shoelaces," I mumbled.

She climbed higher, pulling herself up easily from limb to limb.

"'Cor!" she shouted. "It's great up here. What you can see!"

I nodded. I tried to move my feet but they were glued to the ground.

"What?" she demanded.

What was I going to tell her? That I was scared of heights? That I had nightmares about falling from tall buildings and jumping from bridges? That I woke up in the night covered with sweat, shaken by the dread of something unknown and intangible.

She scrunched up her pudgy face and peered at me through thick bangs of hair that resembled a wet mop.

"You all right, mate?"

I managed a weak nod. Taking a deep breath, I walked closer to the trunk of the tree. I could see the bark, its grooves and lines. I put my hand on it, felt its roughness against my palm.

"Wheee!" Skinner yelled suddenly, jumping up and down on the limb on which she was perched.

"Hey!" I yelled back. "Stop. How d'ya expect me to follow you?"

"Come on! What are ya? A 'fraidy cat!"

I gritted my teeth. Cursed myself for...what? For making a new friend? Showing my weakness? Daring to do something I'd never in my dreams thought I'd do for fun. What? Climb a tree!

I grabbed a sturdy low-hanging branch and pulled myself up as my feet found footholds on the trunk. I reached for the next limb, hoisted my body again, and ascended as easily as if I were climbing a flight of stairs.

"Hey, look! Look at me." I grinned up at her, proud as punch.

But I could only see a glimpse of her through the leaves. She was still climbing.

"Skinner! You daft or something?"

"Come on. This is a great tree to go up. It's easy!"

I was feeling spunky. No more nightmares for me, I thought. Yippeee!

Then I did something I should never have done. I looked up, I looked down. And the ground tilted and swam before my eyes. Waves of nausea threatened to engulf me. I gulped in air, swallowed hard. Willed my numb fingers to keep their grip on whatever lifeline I was clutching. I squeezed my eyes shut and listened to the sound of my own ragged breathing.

Yat-yee-sam-say-ng-luk. Yat-yee-sam-say-ng-luk.

One-two-three-four-five-six. I counted out loud. One-two-three-four-five-six. Seven-eight-nine-ten. One...

At see, at see, where is he?
Where is he?
At see. At see.
He is at see.
Gone.
At see.
Gone to the see.
Gone.

I tried to picture my father's face. Eyes so dark they looked like black wells. Bushy eyebrows. Skin with a covering of freckles. Stubbled cheeks. An image floated into my mind. I was four or five perhaps. Had climbed onto his lap to kiss him goodnight. My lips touched his skin and I remembered my surprise at the feel of the prickly stubble of his cheeks. That was how many years ago? And it was the only memory I had of him.

"Mummy, mummy, where's dad?"

Mother never answered. She pretended not to hear.

"Mummy!"

Mother acted like she was in another world. I didn't know it then, but she was.

I don't know how long it was before I came back to my body. Alison had descended and was now close to me, perched on a neighboring limb, eyes wide.

"You scared me!" she whispered, her voice low and spooked.

"Sorry, I...I don't know what happened."

"You look like you saw a ghost. I shouted at you and you didn't hear me."

"I've got to go home," I mumbled. "I've got to go."

"All right. But we'll play again, eh?"

I nodded uncertainly.

We did play again. Despite our inauspicious beginning, we forged a friendship that summer that endured until high school graduation. She planned to attend secretarial school. I emigrated to the United States.

It was the Friday evening rush hour, and I stood swaying on a crowded Muni streetcar as it lurched up Market Street toward the Castro and home. I was thinking about what I wanted for dinner. Living alone had its advantages. There was no scheduled dinnertime and one could eat whatever one wanted: cold pizza, hot cereal, rice with every meal. The last woman with whom I had a relationship was a confirmed Round Eye, and a white bread midwesterner at that; she used to make fun of my wanting rice for every meal.

I tried to remember what was in the refrigerator and failed. I thought I would duck into the South China Cafe, the Chinese place on Eighteenth, the one that had wooden paneled booths and a waiter who chattered to me in Cantonese, pleased that I was such a Westernized Chinese.

Hong Kong steak cubes with Chinese greens over rice sounded good. Just at that moment the streetcar lurched suddenly and a man jostled against me. He apologized, and I murmured something. I looked up at him as he stood a head above me. It was then I noticed the poster alongside the advertising that ran above the windows.

Lost: Alison Skinner. White female, early thirties. Last seen leaving a Walgreens in the Haight. Wearing blue jeans and a baggy green sweater. A telephone number followed.

For some reason I shuddered, a prescient feeling of gloom settling on me like a heavy cloak. She had been my best friend while I was growing up. But that was in England some twenty odd years ago. The peculiar thing was that I had just been thinking about her that morning.

After dinner at the Chinese place I went straight home even though I had planned to stop at Cala Foods and pick up groceries. I took off my jacket and saw the red light on my answering machine blinking at me.

"Hey, Choy," a voice hailed me.

A shiver arrowed down my back. It had been twenty years, but I'd have recognized the voice anywhere.

"It's Skinner and I'm in trouble."

TO BE CONTINUED...

TO THE FLAMES

JESS WELLS

How do you live when you've been through the flames and your solar plexus has melted inside you like pork rinds on a fire?

I have lived for nearly four hundred years now. Oh, I can hear your skepticism, but I was given a potion by my mother. I'm still not certain if it was wickedness or protection on her part. Either way, time and the linear universe are no match for the ferocious intentions of a woman with a mission. Believe me, I have seen four hundred years of the worst of women. I kept the drug in a pouch in my cleavage, splashing it on the tip of my tongue in moments of utter desperation as I struggled across Europe with a donkey cart of contraband manuscripts. That drug has brought me here, a stooped, haggard old woman, who somehow will not wither and go away—a murderer; a hero; a patron saint of medicine, some say; an enemy of the Church most certainly. The truth is I am a woman whose heart and sense of safety were burned out of her chest when she was a child, who was taught to be who she wasn't and hide when she could, ordered to take my icy heartlessness and use it to vindicate the slaughter of women as witches.

Do I have your pity? I want your rage.

SALERNO, ITALY/1423

My mother was a medical student at the university in Salerno, a port town filled with merchants, scholars, pirates, doctors, and the sick. The healing spas were nearby. The city was choked with schools. Mostly, though, it was a town filled with manuscripts. Books of alchemy and herbalism that came from the Arabs. Books of healing arts and medicine in many languages. Scrolls. Notes bound in boxes, journals, and tomes. All translated and re-copied by the Jewish scribes who plied a quiet trade amid the kinetics of a cosmopolitan seaport. In the offices of the scribes that were scattered throughout the city, men and women clustered and debated the accuracy of the translation, the ideas that emerged from the hidden languages, the healing that might be wrought.

Years later I came to understand that it was a town filled with an unusual breed of woman. The Muslims wouldn't let men provide medical attention to their women, so they educated women to be doctors in Salerno. Jews weren't allowed in universities anywhere else, so Jewish women studied there. The Christians wouldn't educate their women on any subject at all outside of the convent, so Salerno became the one place where women could congregate and study, could move through the city with books in their arms without raising suspicion. The women medical students were world-renowned; they became doctors to kings, founders of hospitals, authors of texts that schooled generations. They studied the medical and gynecological texts of Trotula, indisputably the finest herbalist and medical practitioner in Europe, whose work was the foundation for six hundred years of gynecological knowledge. She had been one of the outstanding professors of the university in 1050 AD. And I'm proud to say that my life has been spent in her service.

Sooner or later, all the women students wound up in front of my mother's fire, debating the merits of this tincture or that procedure. They ate at our table as my mother grew from a student of philosophy and literature to a medical student, then an intern to a physician, and finally to a professor. By the time I was born, though, women doctors already faced a dangerous life, which was discussed late at night in front of the fire, the shadow of the flames dancing across the women's faces like premonition, like doubt. I was just a little girl twirling my thick black hair around my finger when the women first whispered in my mother's private study, in front of her small fire, with her books and papers spilling around us. I would curl my scrawny, birdlike body onto a lambskin rug in front of the fire, staring at the map of Europe pinned to the wall, and my mother would flop into a high-back chair, rubbing her ankles or jotting notes to herself that had nothing to do with the discussion.

Mother's friends would pace the floor, or poke at the fire. Getting worse, they would say. Much worse. The only medical college left for women, they would add, recounting another university closing its doors to women and Jews. Jobs denied even the best of them. This witch thing. An outrage. But we women are doctors, someone would wail. Surely it wouldn't visit itself on us. Several of the queens of Europe had opened hospitals, had trained nurses by the hundreds. Scores of women students from Salerno were finding work in the hospitals.

A woman would stand abruptly, wave her arguments away with her own heated anger. But what about the mass burning of midwives in Provence, in Spain, in the Alpine regions, the woman would wail. What possessed these people to do it? It was as if no one wanted to know anything about medicine. Surgery is what they called it now. Medical quackery on a criminal scale by the men who ignored the teachings of the herbalists. Can you imagine that they only believed in leeches and the knife? Even the teachings of the great Trotula will not be immune. The women would break into argument. Burnings. Savagery.

"Not in front of the child," my mother warned, looking up from her papers. The women would begin their pacing again.

"Who knew she was here," a woman would mutter. "She's like a shadow, this child."

Perhaps it was then that all my childhood games became preparation for this task. I was a shadow, a raven with bristly dark hair, dark eyes, spindly limbs that could fold into crevices and corners. I could see my mother's steely eyes looking at me, trying to find a safe path for her daughter. It made sense in this age to teach a daughter the finer points of stealth. When I was six, mother began giving me small objects and telling me to hide them on myself, to go through the city and deliver them to her friends, undetected. I hid them in my waistband. I encountered mother's friends along the way who tried to ferret out the objects. We would laugh together as they pulled up collars and dug into my pockets, guessed the treasure's whereabouts, applauded my skill. I got sweets and hot buns every time I returned home without my package being detected.

But one summer day during my eighth year, my mother gave me a wooden box to carry that was wider than my chest and very heavy. I was hot, thirsty, sick of the game, and I wrapped the box hastily in a shawl to pretend to be lumbering through the city with a baby. I was halfway to my destination when my mother seemed to come out of nowhere. She pulled me by my arm into a dark corner of a lane.

"This is not a joke," she hissed into my face. "There is no opportunity to let down your guard. Remember at eight and a half you are old enough."

She disappeared into the damp recesses of the streets and I trembled, then sat on the box and cried. By the age of eight and a half the Church could burn you as a witch; you were no longer a little girl. We all knew it—I had only a few months left. When my mother came into my room that evening, her hair loose and long, her face red from crying, she held me in her arms, but nothing could change the calendar.

"I'm so sorry," she whispered, "but you must be smart. I wouldn't have them hurt you for the world."

I have to believe that she meant to hide me, to give me the skills to slip through the net of this time. I can't believe that she trained me only as a messenger, to deliver the secrets but lose my life. Little leather pouches, tiny vials, bits of paper. Soon I learned to hide them in my hair, in my shoes. I became adept at disguises. I developed a keen ability to disappear. I knew the back alleys, the hidden portals, the empty barrels big enough to hide in, the way to double back, to vanish. To drop the item and elude the interceptor, then to return, collect, and deliver. My mother's friends began to tell stories of the complexity of my plans. They trusted me with money, with opiates for childbirths that would land us in a dungeon if found. The items grew larger as my skill increased, until I could run through the city in a summer slip, concealing a book in my clothes. I became a shape-shifter, an amorphous person. Dressed like a boy. Like a fat lady. Like a farmer with stinking bundles who could pass by even my mother's oldest friends undetected. Wearing a gunny-sack shawl and a filthy face, now nearly ten years old but stooped and tiny like an old man, I moved about the city delivering multiple bundles in an increasingly complex web of pickups, deliveries, double switchbacks, and evasion.

In the fall of my tenth year, my mother came around the corner with her friends and I approached them in a beggar's disguise, holding out my hand. This would be the test. Her friends chided the beggar, but my mother reached her hands on either side of my hood, clasped my face, and bent down to kiss me with her buttery warm lips and smell of bread. I had lost the challenge, but my heart lifted to her. For all the rest of my too-long life I would yearn to feel what I knew that moment, that no matter who I became or what I did, my mother could reach in and bring me back to myself.

Later that year she apprenticed me to a scribe. To me, it was as thrilling as any chase through the streets. It sparked, it was alight. I had a decent hand. I knew how to read and write. I was obedient, and a person whose gender could not immediately be guessed, so they tolerated me in the back of the room, sitting like them on a stool behind a tall, narrow desk, laboriously scratching quill across paper.

And the women students at the university insisted that I be the scribe for the works of Trotula. I could track their conversation and the debates in my mother's study against the remedies I had copied a thousand times. I could challenge my memory and sometimes even interject. I became a voracious collector of medical information. I started to follow at the heels of the doctors, usually undetected, dogging them with a little notebook and the stub of a pencil, taking notes, writing down remedies, then checking them at night against Trotula. I jotted down a new way to make a poultice, how one woman steeped leaves and another scorched. My mother introduced me to everyone she knew and asked them to allow me to be a witness.

But I didn't have the gift of healing. The doctors saw the needy line the streets and could sense their illnesses. I was simply a gatherer of facts, a recipe holder, and in some ways I have grown to be grateful for that. If I had been any more compassionate, the life that presented itself in my path would have flung me off a cliff in fury. As it was, I began a life of collecting and archiving, of preserving in a world hellbent on dissipating and forgetting.

On the night of my twelfth birthday, a pattern began that I would live with the rest of my life: a lone woman arrived late at night, battered and wet. There was a gathering of women when everyone should be in bed, then great moaning and frenzied packing. This time my mother packed me. Packed my clothing, packed up my childhood, put the reigns of a donkey-drawn cart in my hands and sent me out of her life.

"You have one hundred manuscripts of the medical knowledge of Trotula," she whispered to me. "Here is a list of their destinations. They're scattered over the Continent, but don't stop until you have delivered them all. You know your map well. I don't doubt you'll find the locations, but you have to be smart, Kore. Don't ever let anyone find them on you." She put her forehead against my cheek and cried.

"Come with me," I whispered.

"Too suspicious. You can do this. Don't tell anyone who I am or where I live. I'll join you when this is over. Kore, be a man in your body and a woman in your soul," she whispered, putting a boy's cap on my head. "A man in danger and a woman in love," she whispered.

She put a small vial with a leather thong around my neck. "Take a few drops of this when the sadness is too great."

She smacked the donkey's ass and we lurched forward. "Always with you...," she called, and as I turned to cry to her, I saw two men try to take her by the arms. She pulled away from them, but didn't turn back to me or answer my cries. No reason she should. In days such as those, who had the luxury of worrying over a little girl's tears?

Trained in subterfuge, medicine, and espionage, I began my life. I headed north, to Rome.

ROME/1424

By the time I approached Rome, the manuscripts were hidden under boards in the bottom of the wagon. I had cut off my hair once and for all, donned the clothes of a boy, and had passed through more than one village as a spindly old man with a bandaged face and shaded eyes. It was too dangerous to be a young girl and too suspect to be an old woman. I bemoaned the fact that there were only two genders and three ages to be—young and vulnerable, adult and dangerous, old and suspect. I yearned to travel the countryside as a dog or a stallion. At night, at least, I could simply curl up as a sheep, or burrow like a wood rat in the hay. I hauled straw and chickens to earn my dinner, shoveled great lumps of manure from the back of my contraband wagon, and lay night after night wishing my mother would hold my cheeks in her long, thin hands.

At the outskirts of Rome, I hid all but ten manuscripts deep in the root cellar of a midwife who regarded the parcels as apparitions. She fed and washed me, held me in her arms while I slept, and I considered giving up, staying there as her child. But my mother said she would join me when I had finished. I was driven to deliver the packages, as I had done for her nearly every day since I was six years old, and return home for hot buns and cider. Who were those men who grabbed her arms? It was a torment to not know if she was in danger. I sipped a few drops from her vial and slept fitfully, rose before dawn, and left.

Rome was a jumble, and I disguised myself in a raggedy old cape and crouched in corners to gain the time to make my way through so many people, down so many strange streets. My game of cat and mouse in my mother's town had made me keen to the whereabouts of priests and guards, until I could look across the town square and watch them moving through the city as if threaded to one another. Sometimes I would climb to the belfry of the university and see their movements as a tapestry; I was the shuttle that would run undetected through their waft. But in Rome there were so many of them that I felt overwhelmed, unable to discern their pattern.

And all over town I saw the evidence of the campaigns that had been the subject of nervous discussions in my mother's house. Rooms were empty that should have housed a midwife who was to receive a package, perhaps give me another morsel of information (plus a roof and a meal, I always hoped). Doors were slammed in my face. Women at addresses I was certain were correct let their eyes glaze over and their voices raise as they denied knowing the woman I sought, or knowledge of my mother.

After I was jostled down a flight of stairs and thrown onto the street, I learned to follow women, to make silent contact across a marketplace, then slip the manuscript into their basket. Or to confront them on the street, jumping out of a dark corner and pretending to beg for money. Better to accost them as a crazy old man than have a learned discussion with them as women. At this rate, it would take me a month to deliver just the manuscripts that were destined for Rome. It was upside down, I knew, but it was in Rome that I first learned the backward would prevail, the life-seekers would succumb.

I turned a corner, six manuscripts left, and four doctors to contact, when there was a great rumbling. I looked up at the buildings that surrounded me, expecting them to break loose. The entire city seemed to be still for a moment, and my chest clenched: my disguises and my ability to slip undetected required my being able to sense ahead of time what was to transpire. But now I stood completely still, my guard down. The square cleared, people ran down the five narrow streets that converged on the piazza. Horse-drawn wagons, the wooden wheels as high as a tall man's head, the sides made of freshly stripped logs, rumbled up the cobblestones. The horses strained against their load, stamping the ground and dislodging stones. Men rushed in with bundles of branches, then unloaded enormous mounds of wood and built a pyre. The sound of women crying echoed off the narrow stone walls. I huddled into a corner behind a rain barrel. I lost track of time.

The next set of wagons held women, some crumpled naked on the bottom, some tied to the slats with their arms straining above their heads. I couldn't be seeing this, not women bloodied and broken, with bones showing and knives still in their flesh. The bodies were piled on one another in the carts like a slaughterhouse parade, and behind the carts, the shackled and crying women in a great horde, more women in one place than in any village I had ever seen. Up the other street came a similar procession, some women with necks still encased in spiked collars that dug into their flesh, stains from the rapists on their clothing, blood pouring onto the pavement.

I thrashed, I turned. I tried to cover my face, my ears, my life from witnessing, from discovery. The women were corralled and the fires lit. The city went mad with screaming, with vengeance, with the stench of burning flesh.

You know this time. You remember it in the muscles of your neck, behind your ears where you hear the past. A bawdy time, you think. When women were wenches with barely covered bosoms, as they sat on men's laps in the oil-lamp dark. Merry laughter. The innkeeper's daughter. When ale slopped out of pewter mugs and wine was grog from goblets. Codpieces, oxen over muddy roads, and houses with thatch roofs. Straw beds, roasted pigs, filth in the house bucket. Rakes and spades of wood, the sickle, the basket. The madness of Bruegel. It is considered a time of superstition, when a few witches were strung up for devil worship. A few scapegoats. But this messenger is here to tell you about one million women murdered. That's right. One million over a span of four hundred years.

I was there in Heidelberg for the mass burning in 1446, in Cologne for the burning in 1456, in Como in 1485 and Metz in 1488. And the cats that were thrown on the pyre of the burning women were no longer able to kill the rats that brought the Black Plague, and so another third of the population was gone. Imagine what one old messenger with nine lives has seen. Much more than grog and goblets. Women tortured and murdered for ministering sophisticated herbal remedies, for defying a profession that would say the knife and the leech was a better medicine, that only men could go to school for medicine and only the schooled could practice. For defying a medicine that was crude and brutal and ignorant. For practicing gynecology of any kind.

And then the fever catching on in the 1500s, and women of

all descriptions killed. Women with money taxed for the trials that would find them guilty, burned at the stake, and their estates then confiscated by the Church. Women burned for defiance. For owning a piece of land. For practicing the ancient reverence for the earth, for goddess worship, for being a pagan, for being a Christian who respected the earth and the seasons, for arguing with her husband, for being in the wrong place in the wrong century. For falling prey to a madman, to Joseph Spenger, whose name is not common knowledge now, but whose sexual perversity and twisted hatred established a textbook for killing that would instruct an army of men in the rigorous extermination of women. The textbook that was responsible for the height of the witch burnings in the 1500s. In some cases, all the women of entire villages killed except for one, and I admit that when I arrived I had to turn away from the survivor's eyes; the loneliness would turn to madness soon enough, I knew.

It was a watershed time. When the great river of women's strength and knowledge was diverted into death, when the gene pool of accomplishment was wiped out, when only the meek survived.

Of course, my mother would chide me for such a statement, because this is a story of survival. Not just my survival, a mixed blessing though it has been. I tell you a story of smuggling. Of flight. Of the women who slipped through their net and lived to rise again. Who are rising still. A story of slow triumph, at great cost.

The world wrenched itself into a horrid shape in the years following that mass burning in Rome. I cowered on the seat of my donkey cart, heading across Europe toward the manuscripts' destinations as fast as I dared, unable to turn back. I wanted to run home, sniveling like a child, but my mother had trained me well. There was a job to do, and I would not let them destroy our body of knowledge. But there were dead women around every turn. Three hanging from a single tree, their tongues dangling and their children crying at their feet. Two butchered just out-side their doors. Four in the village square with their cats strung up beside them. There were too many dead women for me to hang on to hope. Too many of the manuscript recipients carried off to the churches, to the jails, too many whose corpses now stood like blackened matchsticks in what had once been the marketplace. The doctors and midwives were headed to Ireland, I heard on the road. Had my mother begun the journey? The smell in the air said that all the medical knowledge of a hundred years had been extinguished. That the lessons of Trotula could not possibly make their way into the future.

They had almost wiped us out, and those who were left cowered in their root cellars where they would probably stay, picking at invisibilities on their aprons and wringing their hands. I pulled my tattered cloak closer around me, unable to stop shaking. That's where we all will stay. Cowering. Hiding. Careful of our words. Silent more than not. Money that we have stitched into the hems of our skirts or the boundaries of our lives as dangerous as sin. Our property hidden behind the names of our sons. Voices to be raised against our husbands catching in our throats. Life without men lived only in the convent.

The smell of these fires will linger in our lungs for generations. I knew it then, a little girl guiding my donkey cart through the carnage. I know it now, so many years since. It is a smoke that follows us down dark streets at night. We smell it on the hands of the doctor, the priest; we see it hanging over our weddings, our childbirths. It is a racial memory for women. Deep in our skin we remember. And across the torment of having lived too many years, I see it in women—a sudden flinch around the eyes, a careful step, a whisper only just heard. We remember, somewhere in our bodies, in our dreams, in the way we hold our children. We remember that they have hunted us down like rogue pigs for the roasting.

For me, though, it became a flight without destination, running away from something with a terror in my chest that didn't go away. Every day the run sharpened my eyes. I felt the stench of their breath on my neck and I knew that even if I turned around and they weren't there yet, they would be soon enough. Their ferocious pursuit had turned me from a girl into a sinew, a muscle that had no life except to jerk and flinch and contract at the thought of them. No one knew them as I did. No one understood the lengths to which they would go. And because of that damn first gift of herbs, I would see the lengths far longer than anyone should.

If I had known that the drug I prized as my mother's last kiss would turn me into the black cat, wicked target and consort, possessed of (or doomed to) nine lives, I would have spat the mixture she had given me onto the cold stones of the street and escaped. Fled with just one life to lose. And, perhaps, that would have been a gift. To die just once at their hands. Instead, she had enlisted me as the slave of the herb, forced me to stay fully awake and running, to become a death-defying banshee who would lunge at them with a sword that could not be dulled and a body that tortured me with too many sights, too many sorrows, too much hatred. I would live to tolerate too much. And even though I had escaped, they had taken over my vision of the world. They lived inside my mind so fully that even now I wake up in the night with my donkey cart and manuscripts beside me, begging the visions to kill me where I sleep. I was already dead, already destroyed by them, and so it made sense that I should spend my days on the road, planning a way to butcher Joseph Spenger, and every bishop I could find.

TO BE CONTINUED...

ABOUT THE AUTHORS

LUCY JANE BLEDSOE is the author of the novel *Working Parts,* winner of the 1998 American Library Association Gay/Lesbian/ Bisexual Book Award, and of *Sweat: Stories and a Novella* (both from Seal Press). She has also written two novels for young people, *Tracks In The Snow* and *The Big Bike Race* (both from Holiday House). Her short stories have appeared in many publications, including *New York Newsday, Fiction International,* and *Northwest Literary Forum.* She is the editor of *Lesbian Travels: A Literary Companion* and *Gay Travels: A Literary Companion* (both from Whereabouts Press) and a book of erotica, *Heatwave* (Alyson Publications).

NISA DONNELLY is the author of the Lambda Award-winning novel *The Bar Stories,* and *The Love Songs Of Phoenix Bay* (both from St. Martin's Press). She is editor of the recently released *Mom: An Anthology Of Lesbians Writing About Their Mothers* (Alyson Publications). Her work has appeared in numerous anthologies, including *Queer View Mirror* and *Hot & Bothered.* After living in San Francisco for many years, she recently moved two hundred miles to the north.

Jewelle Gomez is the author of four books: a new collection of short fiction, *Don't Explain; Forty-Three Septembers* (essays); a novel, *The Gilda Stories,* winner of two Lambda Literary Awards (Fiction and Science Fiction); and *Oral Tradition: Selected Poems, Old & New* (all from Firebrand). Her work has been frequently anthologized in both academic and trade titles. She is the Executive Director of the San Francisco State Poetry Center and Archives.

Judith Katz is the author of two novels, *Running Fiercely Toward A High Thin Sound,* which won a Lambda Literary Award for Lesbian Fiction, and *The Escape Artist* (both from Firebrand). She teaches in the University of Minnesota Women's Studies Department and Hamline University's graduate MFA/MALS program. She is currently working on a third novel.

Randye Lordon is originally from Chicago. She moved to New York to pursue an acting career and, having discovered that rejection is much easier through the mail, she began writing. Her third Sidney Sloan mystery, *Father Forgive Me* (Avon), won the most recent Lambda Literary Award in that category. It was preceded by *Brotherly Love* and *Sister's Keeper* (St. Martin's), and will be followed shortly by *Mother May I.* She is currently developing a mystery/art CD/ROM game, as well as completing a novel that moves out of the mystery genre and focuses on greed, the root of all humor.

Linda Nelson is a writer and editor as well as Chief Information Officer for Stern Publishing, which includes the *Village Voice* and *LAWeekly* newspapers. Her poetry, prose, and short fiction have been included in several periodicals and anthologies. She lives in Brooklyn, New York.

Elisabeth Nonas is the author of three novels, *For Keeps, A Room Full of Women,* and *Staying Home* (all from Naiad), and co-author with Simon LeVay of the nonfiction *City Of Friends: A Portrait Of The Gay And Lesbian Community In America* (M.I.T. Press). After eighteen years in Los Angeles, she now lives in Ithaca, New York, where she teaches screenwriting at Ithaca College.

CECILIA TAN is the author of *Black Feathers: Erotic Dreams* (HarperCollins) and *The Velderet* (Masquerade), and has edited many anthologies of erotic science fiction and fantasy for Circlet Press, the publishing house she founded in 1992. Her stories have appeared in magazines as diverse as *Penthouse* and *MS.,* and in many anthologies, including *Best American Erotica 1998, Queer View Mirror, Hot & Bothered,* and *Dark Angels.*

CARLA TRUJILLO is the editor of *Chicana Lesbians: The Girls Our Mothers Warned Us About,* winner of a Lambda Book Award (Lesbian Anthology) and the Out/Write Vanguard Award for Best Pioneering Contribution to the Field of Gay/Lesbian Lifestyle Literature (Third Woman Press). In addition to editing the recently released *Living Chicana Theory* (Third Woman Press), Trujillo is also the author of various articles on identity, sexuality, and higher education. She works as an administrator in diversity education and advocacy at the University of California, Berkeley. She is working on a novel about identity and survival.

KITTY TSUI is an Asian Pacific lesbian writer. She is the author of *Breathless,* a collection of erotica (Firebrand), and *Sparks Fly* (writing as Eric Norton). Her poetry, short stories, and erotica have been widely anthologized.

JESS WELLS' publications include the anthology *Lesbians Raising Sons* (Alyson Publications), a novel, *AfterShocks,* and two collections of short stories, *Two Willow Chairs* and *The Dress/The Sharda Stories* (all from Third Side Press). Her work has appeared extensively in lesbian, gay, and feminist literary anthologies.

ABOUT THE EDITORS

MICHELE KARLSBERG is a publicist and event planner for the lesbian, gay, and feminist literary community, and has been so for the past ten years. As the curator of the OUTSPOKEN: Gay and Lesbian Literary Series, she continues to help make visible both new and established writers. She feels that her best energy is put behind the voices that need to be heard. She divides her time between New York and San Francisco.

KAREN X. TULCHINSKY is the author of *Love Ruins Everything,* a novel (Press Gang), and *In Her Nature,* a collection of short stories (The Women's Press). She is co-editor of *Tangled Sheets: Stories & Poems Of Lesbian Lust* (The Women's Press), *Queer View Mirror 1 & 2: Lesbian & Gay Short Short Fiction,* and the editor of *Hot & Bothered: Short Short Fiction On Lesbian Desire* (all from Arsenal Pulp Press). Her fiction has appeared in numerous anthologies, including the Lambda Literary Award-winning *Sister & Brother,* as well as *Heat Wave* and *The Femme Mystique,* and has written features and reviews for *Curve, Girlfriends,* and the *Lambda Book Report.* She lives in Vancouver, Canada.